FREEDOM
AND
BOUNDARIES

FREEDOM
AND
BOUNDARIES

A PASTORAL PRIMER ON THE ROLE
OF WOMEN IN THE CHURCH

KEVIN DEYOUNG

Pleasant W rd

ISBN 1-4141-0611-4
Library of Congress Catalog Card Number: 2005910345

To Trisha,
my beautiful bride, and better than I deserve.

TABLE OF CONTENTS

ACKNOWLEDGMENTS

Saying "thank you" is one of the first things we learn as a child. And with good reason. It's one of the most important things we can say, and one of the most enjoyable.

I'm thankful to have served as an associate pastor at First Reformed Church in Orange City, Iowa. It was a nurturing place to start out in ministry, and many of the elders read through an earlier draft of this book and offered helpful feedback. Special thanks to Jim and Mark for providing the resources which enabled this book to be published.

It's a privilege to serve now as the senior pastor at University Reformed Church in East Lansing, Michigan. My fellow elders, especially, have been a great source of encouragement in this project, though I don't claim that they all agree with me. Tim, Bruce, Allan, Pat, Evan, Keith—it's a joy serving with you.

Tom Stark, my predecessor at University Reformed Church, read an earlier draft of the book and made many useful suggestions.

Kim Falconer read the entire manuscript and made hundreds of little corrections, all of which were necessary. This book is tremendously improved because of her careful proofreading. Any remaining flaws are, of course, my sole responsibility.

And to my dear wife, Trisha, and two little boys, Ian and Jacob–thanks for being who you are even when I am not all that I want to be.

INTRODUCTION:
IS THIS BOOK REALLY
NECESSARY?

Do we really need another book about gender roles in the church?

The answer would appear to be "No." There are more books about men and women in the church than probably deserve to be written. I am not a professional academic, and yet, I've read at least a dozen books on the subject in the past five years, and another couple dozen journal articles, and that's not even a fraction of the literature from just evangelical authors. And while I am immensely grateful for the work scholars have done and continue to do on the issue, there does come a point of diminishing returns. There are only so many books (one hopes) that can be written on Galatians 3:28, 1 Timothy 2:12, *kephale*, and *authentein*. After a while, the constant proliferation of books and articles only serves to confuse the "average" Christian and cause him to despair of ever making up his mind on the issue.

It is because of this "No," however, that there is also a "Yes." Real Christians and real churches cannot avoid this issue. I have been a pastor at two different churches, both of which struggled with how to define male and female roles in the church. The first church I served (as an associate pastor) was a large Reformed church in rural Iowa. The official stance taken by the church was "no stance." The pastors and elders, reflective of the entire church, were divided on the issue. To my knowledge, at present, the church's policy could be characterized as "open but not realized." That is, there are no positions of leadership or teaching that are closed to women, but in practice, only men have served as pastors, elders, and Sunday morning preachers.

The church I currently serve (as senior pastor) is a medium-size Reformed church in a university setting in Michigan. Like the church in Iowa, this church, at present, has no official stance on the roles of men and women in the church. Unlike my previous church, however, this one has not been exactly neutral on the subject. My predecessor preached at various times about men and women over the years in his exposition of Scripture. It was no secret that while he affirmed the gifts and ministries of women, he believed elders and preaching pastors should be men.

I share his viewpoint. But some in the church do not. So where do we go from here? What's the right step for churches in similar situations? What should pastors and elders think, and how should they lead their congregations through the stormy sea of gender roles in the church? Answering questions like these is the purpose of this book.

Specific Audience

I have a very specific audience in mind in writing this book: my congregation and others like it. Our church has a book table around the corner from the fellowship hall. I have often wished for a book there that explained the Bible's teaching about men and women in the church in a way that the interested layperson could understand and in a size that one could read in a few hours. I have wished for a book that would argue its case without being argumentative; a book I could give to other pastors wrestling with this issue, and a book pastors could give to their elders, deacons, and trustees that they would actually read; a book that displayed exegetical integrity with minimal technical jargon; a book weightier than a pamphlet, but lighter than a door stop. I'm not sure I've written such a book, but this is the book I set out to write.

Complementarian Perspective

I do not write this book hesitating between two opinions. I am a convinced complementarian. *Complementarians* believe that men and women are equal in value but have different and complementary roles in the home and in the church. *Egalitarians*–those on the opposite side of the debate in the evangelical world—believe that full equality entails the removal of any gender-based role distinctions in the home or in the church. The terms are cumbersome and not all use them, but I know of no better terminology. "Complementarian" carries less baggage than "traditional," "patriarchal," or "hierarchical." And "egalitarian" seems fairer than "progressive," "liberal," or "feminist."

As a complementarian, I believe that God's design is for men to lead, and that, in the church, women should not teach, or have authority over them. I will try to show from the Bible that this is the case, what this means, and why it matters.

Irenic Spirit

It goes without saying, that I hope to make a convincing case for the complementarian position. Authors do not write books unless they want to persuade people. But besides convincing, I also hope my case is considerate. The Lord's servant "must not be quarrelsome but kind to everyone, able to teach, patiently enduring evil, correcting his opponents with gentleness" (2 Tim. 2:24-25). My aim is to treat others, whether in person or in writing, as I would want to be treated—fairly, honestly, and with respect. Even as I write, I see in my mind the faces of friends, family, and co-laborers I love who don't see eye to eye with me on this issue. I may disagree with their position, but I do not want to disparage their person or demean their piety.

I assume that egalitarians love the family and love the church. And because I am writing for other evangelicals, I assume that those who are not persuaded by my arguments nevertheless love the Bible. To be sure, I have known unthinking, culturally-captive egalitarians whose support for "women in ministry" is based on precious little biblical reflection. But I have also known unthinking, belligerent complementarians who agree with me for all the wrong reasons. Loving like Jesus demands that we don't argue against the worst examples from either camp. So I will assume that pastors and laypersons reading this book believe the Bible and are eager to do what it says.

Intelligent, Yet Readable

My desire is to put into the hands of churches struggling with this issue a work that is intelligent and readable. In hopes of being an intelligent help for congregations, I work through the pertinent Scripture passages, including several chapters of fairly detailed exegesis, and a smattering of (transliterated) Greek words. In hopes of being readable, I have tried to be concise, brief, and informed of the current scholarship without getting bogged down in footnotes except where attribution is demanded.

Those interested in reading more can consult the best door-stop books on both sides:

Complementarian

John Piper and Wayne Grudem, eds., *Recovering Biblical Manhood & Womanhood: A Reponse to Evangelical Feminism* (Wheaton: Crossway, 1991), 566 pages. The standard text for the complementarian position.

Andreas J. Köstenberger, Thomas R. Schreiner, and H. Scott Baldwin, eds., *Women in the Church: A Fresh Analysis of 1 Timothy 2:9-15* (Grand Rapids: Baker, 1995), 334 pages. A thorough analysis of the most disputed text. An updated, streamlined second edition is also worth consulting. Andreas J. Köstenberger and Thomas R. Schreiner, eds., *Women in the Church: An Analysis and Application of 1 Timothy 2:9-15* (Grand Rapids: Baker Academic, 2005), 287 pages.

Wayne Grudem, *Evangelical Feminism & Biblical Truth: An Analysis of More Than One Hundred Disputed Questions* (Sisters, Oregon: Multnomah, 2004), 856 pages. Attempts to answer every conceivable egalitarian objection.

Egalitarian

Craig S. Keener, *Paul, Women and Wives: Marriage and Women's Ministry in the Letters of Paul* (Peabody, MA: Hendrickson, 1992), 350 pages. A thorough, well documented look at Paul's letters which argues for a culturally relative reading of the pertinent texts.

William J. Webb, *Slaves, Women, and Homosexuals: Exploring the Hermeneutics of Cultural Analysis* (Downers Grove, IL: IVP, 2001), 301 pages. Maintains that the Christian ethic on women and slavery follows the trajectory of the Bible past the New Testament, while the ethic for homosexuality is found in the New Testament itself.

Ronald W. Pierce, Rebecca Merrill Groothuis, and Gordon D. Fee, eds., *Discovering Biblical Equality: Complementarity Without Hierarchy* (Downers Grove, IL: IVP, 2004), 528 pages. A response to *Recovering Biblical Manhood and Womanhood*; probably will become the standard text for the egalitarian position.

CHAPTER ONE

SETTING THE STAGE

Before we consider anything else about men and women in the church, there are several questions that must be answered and a number of balances that must be struck.

Question 1: What do we already know?

A lot. We know that Christ calls us to humility before himself and others. We know that our relationships must be marked by love and gentleness. We know that we worship a God of grace, and we ourselves are saved by grace alone.

We also know that truth matters. Sound doctrine was a concern for the early church and it is our goal today. We know that the Bible is the final arbiter between right and wrong—both for doctrine and godliness. The Bible makes no mistakes. If we listen to the Spirit speaking through the Word we will be safe from error.

We know that Jesus Christ is the only King and Head of his church. We know that Jesus rose from the dead. We know that he is coming again. We know how to live as we fix our eyes on Jesus, who came from the Father full of grace and truth. We are already convinced of and agree on many important points of biblical theology and practice.

Question 2: Is this a "salvation issue"?

Of course not. There are certain truths and propositions one must believe in order to be saved (see for example 1 John 2:18-27; 5:1-13). Complementarianism is not one of those truths. Faith in Jesus Christ is a salvation issue. The divinity of Jesus Christ is a salvation issue. Unrepentant, unchecked ungodliness is a salvation issue.

Baptism is not a salvation issue. Our understanding of the millennium is not a salvation issue. And the role of women in the church is not a salvation issue. Its urgency and importance do not match that of the Trinity, the resurrection, the uniqueness of Christ, or a host of other matters.

Question 3: Should we care about "non-salvation issues"?

Yes. In fact, we already do. Many churches adhere to confessions that delineate with precision things like God's providence, original sin, election, the extent of the atonement, church discipline, baptism, the Lord's Supper, reprobation, irresistible grace, and the perseverance of the saints. Entire denominations are built upon non-salvation issues. Every week preachers preach about non-salvation issues. And year after year, churches try to make wise decisions on hundreds of non-salvation issues, from the mundane–where to put the nursery–to the controversial–what style of music to have. We never have, and never will, limit ourselves only to those things that are absolutely essential to getting our ticket punched for heaven.

And for good reason. We are not salvation minimalists. That is, we are not interested in only the bare minimum necessary to get out of hell. We are interested in glorifying God as fully and faithfully as possible. We want to speak where the Bible has spoken. If the Bible says something about predestination, we want to say something about predestination. If the Bible says something about gender, we want to say something about gender.

Remember Paul's words to the Ephesian elders: "I did not shrink from declaring to you the whole counsel of God" (Acts 20:27). What did Paul do in Ephesus for three years? He did more than get people "saved;" he declared the whole counsel of God. He was less interested in getting decisions for Christ, and more interested in making disciples. His strategy was a far cry from some evangelists in our day who are only concerned to share the minimum amount of truth to the maximum number of people. Paul, on the other hand, stayed with the Ephesians for three years (Acts 20:31), declaring anything that was profitable and teaching in public and from house to house (Acts 20:20). When Paul lectured for two years in the hall of Tyrannus (Acts 19:9-10), surely he taught more truth than can be put on a one-page statement of faith. His aim was to build his converts into communities which understood the breadth and depth of biblical teaching and living. He wanted the maximum amount of truth for the maximum number of people.

If we limited our concern to "salvation issues" we would have very little to do outside the church. We would not get passionate about most political issues. We would not work for improvement in our schools. We would not insist upon excellence in our jobs. Our salvation does not depend upon presidential candidates, academic excellence, or vocational improvement, yet we care about these issues (and many others) because they matter to God.

The very fact that God left us on earth after justification suggests that his purpose for our lives is more than to save our souls. He wants us to be agents of redemption in this fallen world. Therefore, our passions and concerns will extend to the arts, science, film, industry, agriculture, theology and every other area of life about which Jesus Christ calls out (as Abraham Kuyper said) "This is mine!" While we don't want to needlessly divide Christians (see Question #5), the grace God shows in saving his sometimes ignorant and mistaken people should not encourage us to declare less than the whole counsel of God.

Question 4: Why should we care about this "non-salvation issue"?

Aye, there's the rub. Just because we should care about non-salvation issues as a general rule, does not mean we should care about every non-salvation issue. There are some issues which should not concern us. Circumcision and uncircumcision mean nothing; certain holy days mean nothing; dietary food restrictions mean nothing. These are not matters of right and wrong, provided one's conscience is not violated.

There are also some issues we can care about too much. One thinks of the false teachers in Timothy's midst who devoted themselves to idle speculation about genealogies and endless debates about Jewish myths. These controversies were not simply unimportant. They were so unimportant as to be dangerous.

Other issues, however, even ones that may not affect our eternal destiny, are worthy of our concern. This is one of those issues. Although we will not be sent to heaven or hell based on our understanding of gender roles in the church, I believe every Christian should wrestle with this issue and come to some conclusions.

In other words, we ought to care about this "non-salvation issue." Here are a few reasons why:

1. There are strong opinions on both sides of the issue in the church. That does not, by itself, mean the issue merits all our attention,

but it does mean that ignoring it would be unwise.

2. Our understanding of the equality and dignity of men and women made in the image of God is at stake.

3. What we think about men and women in the church will shape the marriages we live out in the home.

4. How we understand the relationship between men and women can help us understand or misunderstand the relationship among the Persons of the Trinity.

5. This issue is both a product of and a shaping influence on the way we interpret the Bible. Even among Bible-believing Christians, there are crucial differences in our approach to God's Word. Those differences surface in this debate.

6. We live in a society with rampant gender confusion. Sexuality has run amuck and many of our neighbors, and not a few church members, wonder if male and female are just social constructions. Men do not understand what it means to be a man, if it means anything at all. And women are often left despising their femininity. Regardless of one's position on men and women in the church, as long as we live in a culture which is unsure if men and women are really different in the first place, we need to speak clearly on this issue.

7. The Bible has a lot to say about manhood and womanhood. From Genesis to Jesus to Paul, the Bible talks about marriage and the relationship between the sexes. The discussion of men and women in the home and in the church is not isolated to a single text but occurs in Genesis, Proverbs, Malachi, Matthew, 1 Corinthians, Galatians, Ephesians, Colossians, 1 Timothy, 2 Timothy, Titus, and 1 Peter to name but the main examples. If we refuse to work toward a conclusion on this "non-salvation issue" we are not simply looking past one or two isolated texts, we are ignoring a critical thread that is woven throughout the pages of Scripture.

8. The world outside the church will not ignore this issue. Increasingly, even newcomers to our churches want to know where we stand on this issue and what we believe the Bible teaches about manhood and womanhood.

Question 5: This issue is so controversial. Isn't it just going to cause division in the church?

At least three assumptions go into this question. The first assumption is that controversy is always bad. People getting passionate about opposite sides of an issue, it is presumed, must be avoided at all costs. But controversy does not always mean disaster, just as a cough does not always mean the body is getting sicker. Coughs can make the throat raw, but they can also clear it. Sometimes a cough, though unsettling, is a sign that the body is getting better. In the same way, God often uses controversy to help the church sharpen its focus and clarify its vision. Controversy, because it makes us think more carefully and support our ideas more substantially, can actually strengthen the church.

The second assumption in this question is that making an issue clearer actually causes the division. I would maintain that more clearly defining an issue does not cause new divisions as much as it brings to light existing ones. In most churches, working through this issue may actually help minimize future divisions by bringing to the surface differences of opinion that are already present.

Third, underlying this question is the tacit assumption that disagreement is the same as division. Jesus and Paul warned strenuously against division, but they also vigorously disagreed at times with their disciples and churches. They often critiqued their followers for doing and believing the wrong things, but this did not make them guilty of tearing apart the unity of the church. Division comes primarily from divisive people–those who are puffed up, haughty, arrogant, and disdainful of others. It may be the case that such people exist in our churches (on both sides of the issue), which would be unfortunate. But let us not think that holding strongly to an opinion or even trying to change someone else's mind is the same thing as causing division.

Question 6: Can't we just agree to disagree?

Yes and no. As individuals, we can come to different conclusions and still have genuine fellowship with one another in Christian love and mutual respect. In that sense, we can agree to disagree.

But we can't agree to disagree if agreeing to disagree means we refrain, individually or corporately, from coming to a conclusion on the matter. No doubt, well-meaning people on both sides, in the name of peace and unity, will argue for a "no position" position. This sounds nice–no winners, no losers–but in the end I don't think a "no position" position is tenable (EN 1).

For starters, I don't believe the Bible gives us that option. There is simply too much at stake to write off the whole debate as *adiaphora*–a non-moral matter of liberty. This isn't in the same category as food sacrificed to idols, or meat versus vegetables, or the color of church carpet. This is not a matter of preference or simple administration. This is a rich theological issue rooted in an understanding of creation–the kind of issue the apostle Paul never leaves to conscience alone.

Just as crucially, it is practically impossible to take no position on this issue. Either women will hold positions of teaching/authority in the church or they will not. That much *will* happen. We may be able to allow for diversity within our church, or para-church organization, or Christian institution, but as an official policy "agree to disagree" will not last very long. In my denomination, for example, there are no restrictions on women holding any office, but those who disagree with the official position are not (as of yet anyway) forced to support women's ordination in their own churches. That's one way to agree to disagree, but it is not the same as "no position."

When a church takes no position on this issue, it is usually saying one of three things. The church leadership could be saying, "We don't believe all roles are open to women, but rather than stating that in an official way, we will live by our convictions informally." Or the leadership could be saying, "We may or may not believe there are any gender based restrictions, but we won't press the issue one way or the other." Or, finally, "We don't believe this issue is really important. Whatever happens happens."

I believe all three options, however well-intended in the name of unity, will, over the long run, cause greater division, pushing disagreements underground instead of bringing them to light where they belong. Congregations will be frustrated as a result. With the first option, egalitarians will feel trapped in a policy that doesn't prohibit what they want, but in practice won't allow it. In the other two options, complementarians will feel betrayed as eventually the wait and see approach will yield women in positions of leadership they deem inappropriate. With a topic as controversial as gender roles in the church, I believe the wisest move is for the church leadership to gently but firmly explain what they believe to be the biblical position, while reaching out to those in their midst who disagree.

Balance 1: Honesty and Diligence

Let us be honest before the word of God. Even Peter admitted that certain things in Paul's letters were hard to understand (2 Peter 3:16). The Bible is not always clear to us. We do not have perfect knowledge of the Scriptures. Our understanding of God is sometimes more shadow than substance. We see in part and we know in part.

And let us also be diligent in handling the word of God. The Bereans were not deemed noble because they pleaded ignorance to hard questions, but because they daily searched the Scriptures (Acts 17:11). Humility is one thing; laziness is another. We can learn more. Some questions can be answered. If we surrender every disputed point of theology to the realm of the inconsequential, we will have no faith left at all. We must resist the temptation to throw up our hands in indecision just because there are a lot of books on both sides of the debate. After all, what doctrine don't Ph.D.'s disagree on?

Balance 2: Humility and Conviction

Let us be humble before each other. The Lord's servant must not be quarrelsome. Even in the face of error, Paul commands teachers to correct with gentleness (2 Tim. 2:24-25). No matter what we decide, we will have gotten this issue wrong if we are cantankerous, condescending, and belligerent. Instead, we should respect each other, carefully examining the possible log in our own eye before removing the speck in our neighbor's eye.

And let us also speak with conviction to one another. We should not confuse humility with uncertainty. Moses was humble (more so than any person, according to Numbers 12:3), yet he was filled with passion and conviction, boldness and power. His humility was not antithetical to his love for the truth. Speaking in a direct, frank way is not the same as divisiveness. And belief in the rightness of one's opinion is not the same as pride. Contrary to much of the postmodern rhetoric about mystery and journey, there are higher virtues than ignorance, contradiction, and ambiguity.

Balance 3: Keeping Silent and Speaking Out

Let us allow the Bible to be silent where it is silent. The Bible simply does not address every issue that is of interest to us. We do not know specifics for a lot of things we would really like to know specifically. If the Bible does not give an absolute answer to our question, let's not pretend it does. God's revelation is not impugned in any way when we admit that the Bible is silent on some points.

And let us allow the Bible to speak where it has something to say. The Bible doesn't say everything, but it does say something. Even if our knowledge is imperfect, it does not have to be inaccurate. Our faith will be damaged if we subtly slip into the erroneous idea that the Bible is horribly unclear and without a discernible meaning in the text. Of course we want to have an open mind, but the purpose of an open mind, as G.K. Chesterton remarked, is to close down on something solid (preferably the truth). True open-mindedness is not only the humble awareness of ignorance, but also the desire to fill that ignorance with knowledge.

CHAPTER TWO

THE AUTHORITY AND INTERPRETATION OF THE BIBLE

As I said earlier, I do not assume that my "opponents" in this issue automatically have a lower view of Scripture simply because they disagree with me. We all believe, I hope, that the sixty-six books of the Old and New Testaments are efficient for salvation, sufficient for Christian life and godliness, without error, unique, and complete. While the Bible does not answer all our questions (maybe we need better questions?), it is a safe and sure guide. This much evangelicals can agree on: we share the Reformation conviction that the final and ultimate authority for doctrine, life, and the church is *sola scriptura*.

Principles of Interpretation

The more difficult question is whether we agree on how to interpret the Bible. The issue is one of hermeneutics. That is, what is our interpretive methodology? What sort of principles do we use in order to rightly understand the Bible? I suggest the following seven principles to help frame our approach to Scripture.

First, we ought to pray for illumination from the Holy Spirit. The same Spirit who inspired the Scriptures can help us understand them correctly and live them out fully. This step is not a perfunctory ritual; it is the wind in our sails blowing us toward good interpretation. We desperately need the Spirit to give us humble hearts and teachable minds that we might hear God's voice in the Scriptures.

Second, the best interpretation is done in community. This means we listen to other godly persons who have gifts of wisdom and knowledge. Our learning is to be done within the communion of the saints. We can learn from each other.

And we can learn from those who have gone before us. While our interpretations are not bound to tradition, it always wise to test our conclusions against the history of interpretation so as to avoid chronological snobbery and cultural short-sightedness.

Third, we must pay attention to genre. What kind of book are we reading? Is this poetry, narrative, epistle, parable, etc.? We shouldn't read Psalm 23 the same way we read Romans 8 and we shouldn't read Proverbs the same way we read Revelation.

Fourth, the Bible should be interpreted according to its natural or plain sense. Some would call this the literal meaning, but the word "literal" is so abused and misunderstood that it is more helpful to call this the plain or natural sense. Granted, what is the plain sense to one person may not be so plain to someone else (see the sixth principle below). But reading the Bible in its plain or natural sense means we read it like we would read most any other book. We shouldn't go looking for all sorts of strange allegories or "spiritual" readings or hidden messages. Likewise, we understand in the normal conventions of writing that authors use figures of speech and metaphors and hyperbole. When Jesus said "I am the bread of life," we know he's not calling himself a loaf of wheat and barley. He's simply using language in the dynamic way it has always been used.

Fifth, we should adhere to the analogy of faith. This simply means that we should let Scripture interpret Scripture. Since all of Scripture is God-breathed, it exhibits, even with multiple authorship, an overall coherence and harmony. Scripture does not disagree with Scripture. We need to use the whole of biblical revelation to help us understand the individual parts.

Sixth, we approach the Bible with the belief that we can know the mind of God in the Scriptures. The text means something. Our task is to determine, as humbly and objectively as possible, what that meaning is.

Now some may object: "Doesn't it just come down to one interpretation against another? How can we possibly come to any definite conclusions on the meaning of a text? Both sides of the women's issue, for example, point to the Bible for support. How will we ever reach a conclusion?"

These are fair questions, but we must be careful. There *is* a meaning in the text. The existence of rival meanings does not preclude that one of them is right or at least more correct than another.

Many people use the Bible for their ideas, and yet evangelicals have no problem dismissing them. Some health, wealth, and prosperity preachers use the Bible to promote their lavish lifestyles; cults use the Bible to show that Jesus is not God; homosexuals use the Bible to demonstrate God's unconditional acceptance of their behavior. The truth is that we discount scores of ideas that purport to be based on the Bible. And why? Because we believe they misinterpret the Bible. We've come to a decision that though they use the Bible, they do so wrongly. Granted, there are some issues raised in the Bible that we haven't figured out (like baptisms for the dead in 1 Corinthians 15), but this does not mean we cannot settle any issue. We do not want to be in the same corner with the interpretative relativists. We don't want to take away from biblical authority by declaring that all we have are "interpretations." As soon as we make disagreements nothing more than a dispute between one interpretation against another, we might as well give up on exegesis altogether, not to mention any notion of Truth with a capital "T."

Let's not do to ourselves what our culture has done, namely, relocate religion to the realm of opinion away from the realm of knowledge. The more we talk about competing irreconcilable interpretations, the closer we get to our culture's understanding of religion. In North America, religion is about opinions, values, and beliefs instead of knowledge, virtue, and truth. As a result, instead of thinking more deeply, we simply relativize the things we disagree about most, which tend to be the things that actually matter most. It is possible that the evidence concerning women's ordination is simply inconclusive, but that decision must be reached through a pursuit of the truth, not a relativizing of it. God has purposed to speak to us through the words of Scripture. Therefore, putting aside our biases as much as we humanly can, let's come to the Bible expecting to hear God's voice.

Seventh, in interpreting the Bible, we must try to separate what is normative (true for all people at all times in all places) from what is non-normative (true only for a specific people at a specific time in a specific place). I think we all agree that biblical commands are in most cases normative, but not always. Abraham left his homeland to follow God, but many of us stay put. God commanded Noah to build an ark, but we don't build arks. Yet, we think that Jesus' command to the disciples to love their neighbors applies to us. What's the difference? It won't do to simply say that some things recorded in the Bible aren't normative (everyone agrees on that) and say therefore that this particular text (whatever it might be) shouldn't be normative either. Besides being sloppy, this approach leads to exegetical chaos. We must have reasons for calling some things normative and others not.

So how do we know what is normative in the Bible and what isn't? Here are seven questions we can ask to help us determine, not the meaning, but the continuing significance of a given passage (EN 2).

1. *Does the text itself limit the application?* When Paul commands Timothy to "bring the cloak that I left with Carpus at Troas" (2 Tim. 4:13), we in no way think God wants all of us to look for Paul's cloak at Troas (or worse yet, look for Carpus!). The specificity of the text limits its own application.

2. *Does subsequent revelation limit the application?* This is often the case when moving from the Old Testament to the New. Most Christians are confused as to why we "ignore" so many commands written in the Old Testament. Instinctively, it seems in some vague way that those commands must have been "cultural." But culture is not so much the answer as is further biblical revelation. Many Old Testament shadows have been fulfilled in New Testament substance. For example, we don't offer animal sacrifices anymore because Hebrews has made clear that Jesus Christ is our once-for-all sacrifice (Heb. 9:11-14). Subsequent revelation has explicitly limited the application of the Old Testament sacrificial system.

3. *Does this specific teaching appear to be in conflict with other biblical teaching?* This is similar to the fifth principle of interpretation (the analogy of faith). A good example of a biblical command that seems to be in conflict with other scriptural teaching is Jesus' command to the disciples: "Do not go among the Gentiles...Go rather to the lost sheep of Israel" (Matthew 10:5-6 NIV). We know from the Great Commission that Jesus later commanded the disciples to go into the whole world with the gospel. The command in Matthew 10 does not contradict Matthew 28, however, so long as we understand that Jesus' initial command was limited to that specific moment in salvation history prior to the full inclusion of the Gentiles into the people of God.

4. *Is this command undergirded by some sort of ongoing, normative rationale?* The Great Commission, again, is a good example. Strictly speaking, Jesus only commanded the disciples with him to go into all the world, yet we read it as our commission too. Why? Because we realize that Jesus is grounding his command in more than a specific time and location. He grounds his command in unchangeable truths like "all authority has been given to me" and "I am with you always, to the end of the age." The latter promise to be with the disciples to the end of the age

necessitates that disciples beyond the original Apostles (who have all died) must continue fulfilling the Great Commission.

5. *Is the specific teaching normative or just the underlying principle?* In other words, does the text state a universal principle and then make a non-universal application? For example, I will argue that Paul, in 1 Timothy 2:9-10, issues a normative command that women dress modestly, but then applies this principle with a non-binding application: no gold, pearls, braids, or costly attire.

6. *Does the Bible treat the historic context as normative?* It can be argued that when Jesus promised that the Holy Spirit would lead the disciples into all truth, it was a promise specifically for the Apostles who would be the foundation of the church (cf. Eph. 2:20). But when Paul tells the Ephesians they were chosen before the foundation of the world (Eph. 1:4), we get no indication that a different historical setting would have elicited a different teaching.

7. *Does the Bible treat the cultural context as limited?* No complementarian that I know of is arguing that we "re-create the first century," as is sometimes alleged. First century customs are not sacrosanct just because they took place in New Testament times. For example, Paul encouraged the believers to "Greet one another with a holy kiss"

(1 Cor. 16:20), and yet little kissing takes place in our churches. Are we disobedient then? No, rather we can see that the cultural context of this command is limited. Elsewhere Paul offers greetings without enjoining holy kissing and sometimes with the right hand of fellowship (Gal. 2:9). Clearly, Paul's holy kiss was one acceptable way of greeting each other, but is not normative for all people at all times.

All of which is to say, that even after we know what the text meant in its original context, there are still more questions to ask before we can understand its ongoing significance. Of course, I am not advocating that we go through seven steps to determine the meaning of a passage and then seven more steps to determine its significance. Such a process would be tedious and mechanical. These methodological principles should serve, not as a formula for arriving at the right interpretation, but as guideposts that keep us on the path toward good exegetical understanding and application.

CHAPTER THREE

GENESIS 1-3

I've heard it said that "All good theology starts in Genesis." That's not far off the mark. In Genesis, we see how God started things. We have the beginning of the story. In the first two chapters of Genesis, God gives us a stunning picture of paradise, a portrait of the good life—the way things were, the way they are supposed to be, and the way they will be again.

In Eden, all was very good. The natural world was good, with its striking beauty and peaceable cooperation. The creation of man—from the dust of the earth to the crown of creation—was good. Work was good. No broken tractors, no thorns and thistles, no computer crashes, no anxious deadlines, no cranky bosses, no incompetent employees, no power plays; just an honest day's work under the smiling face of

God. And the Garden, as a kind of temple in which God's presence dwelt, was good.

But even before the fall, even in this paradise, there was one thing which, if left undone, would not have been good: leaving man alone.

We do not know that Adam was lonely or that he felt isolated in any way. The man didn't complain to God; rather, God declared that his situation was not good. Every other aspect of creation had its counterpart. The day had its sun, the night its moon, the waters its fish, the sky its birds, and the ground its animals, but the man did not have a woman. "So the Lord God caused a deep sleep to fall upon the man, and while he slept took one of his ribs and closed up its place with flesh. And the rib that the Lord God had taken from the man he made into a woman and brought her to the man" (Gen. 2:21-22). This was very good.

Equal in Dignity

And men and women were equal, which was good. The first chapters of Genesis show clearly that from the beginning men and women have been equal in worth, dignity, and honor.

We know this to be true for several reasons. **First, both were created in the image of God.** "So God created man in his own image, in the image of God he created him; male and female he created them" (1:27). Men and women, as distinct from all else in creation, are image-bearers. We are like statues or icons placed in creation to testify to the world that God has dominion over this place.

More important for our concern, as image-bearers, not to mention co-heirs of the grace of life (1 Peter 3:7), men and women possess equal value as human beings. Eve was not a lesser creature. She was not an inferior being. She imaged God as well as Adam did. Although God has revealed himself in masculine language (e.g., Father, King, Husband), he is neither male nor female. To be faithful to God's revelation we should speak of God only in the masculine terms he has given us, but to call God "Father" is not the same as saying God is a man. God does not have a gender. Consequently, maleness is no more holy or divine than femaleness. Both Adam and Eve had equal access to God, and both were equally valuable to God.

Second, male and female were given joint rule over creation. Together they were to replenish the earth and subdue it. To image our Triune God means that human beings, both male and female, are directed toward God, directed toward neighbor, and rule over nature.

Third, the names "man" and "woman" suggest interdependence. In Genesis 2:23, Adam exclaimed "she shall be called Woman [*ishah*], because she was taken out of Man [ish]." The names themselves suggest male and female interdependence. As Paul makes clear, "in the Lord woman is not independent of man nor man of woman; for as woman was made from man, so man is now born of woman" (1 Cor. 11:11-12).

Fourth, the two came from one flesh and became one flesh. Eve was bone of Adam's bone, and flesh of his flesh. In other words, men and women are made of the same stuff and meant for each, not so that one dissolves into the other, but that the two become one. John Calvin sums up well:

> But if the two sexes had proceeded from different sources, there would have been occasion either of mutual contempt, or envy, or contentions...Yet... something was taken from Adam, in order that he might embrace, with greater benevolence, a part of himself. He lost, therefore, one of his ribs; but, instead of it, a far richer reward was granted him, since he obtained a faithful associate of life; for he now saw himself, who had before been imperfect, rendered complete in his wife.
>
> —EN 3

Different Roles

In the paradise of Eden, men and women were created equal. They were also created different. The first chapters of Genesis show just as clearly that men and women–equal in worth, dignity, and honor–were different and enjoyed different roles.

We see this, first, in that man was created before the woman. Whatever we may think of primogeniture (rights of the firstborn) and its bearing on Genesis 2, we cannot help but find some significance in the order of creation. After all, the Apostle Paul, inspired by the Holy Spirit, did. "I do not permit a woman to teach or to exercise authority over a man;

rather, she is to remain quiet. *For Adam was formed first, then Eve*" (1 Tim. 2:12-13, emphasis added).

Second, the woman was given as a helper to the man. She was created *from* man (2:22)–equal in worth–and she was also created *for* man (2:20)–different in function. The male leadership which the text hints at in 1:27 by calling male and female "man" as opposed to "woman," is spoken plainly in chapter two when Eve is given to Adam as his "helper" (2:18, 20). As egalitarians are quick to point out, being a helper carries no connotations of diminished worth or status; for God is sometimes called the helper of Israel. *Ezer* (helper) is a functional term. Just as God at times comes alongside to help his people, so the role of the woman in relationship to her husband is that of a helper. So *ezer* is not a demeaning term. But this does not negate the clear teaching of 2:18, that Eve was given as a helper to Adam, and not the other way around. "For man was not made from woman, but woman from man. Neither was man created for woman, but woman for man" (1 Cor. 11:8).

Eve was to help Adam rule over creation, produce offspring, and support his leadership. In short, woman was given to help man live well. Again, Calvin's remarks are worth quoting:

> Some suppose that a distinction between the two sexes is in this manner marked, and that it is thus shown how much the man excels the woman. But I am better satisfied with an interpretation which, though not altogether contrary, is yet

47

different...The vulgar proverb, indeed, is that she is a necessary evil; but the voice of God is rather to be heard, which declares that woman is given as a companion and an associate to the man, to assist him to live well...For if the integrity of man had remained to this day such as it was from the beginning, that divine institution would be clearly discerned, and the sweetest harmony would reign in marriage; because the husband would look up with reverence to God; the woman in this would be a faithful assistant to him; and both, with one consent, would cultivate a holy, as well as friendly and peaceful intercourse.

—EN 4

Third, man was given the responsibility for naming. Adam named the animals and named Eve too. Moreover, "man" is the name for the human race, male and female, pointing to God-given male leadership.

Fourth, Adam is reckoned as the head and representative of the couple. Adam is given the initial command regarding the tree of the knowledge of good and evil (2:16-17). And even though Eve, tempted by the Serpent, commits the initial crime, Adam is addressed first (3:9). The Lord called to the man and asked, "Where are you?" for Adam was the designated leader and representative. Romans 5 makes this indisputably clear. "Therefore, just as sin came into the world *through one man,* and death through sin, and so death spread to all men because all sinned" (Rom. 5:12, emphasis added). In other words, Adam, not Eve, was the federal head.

But before we get too far into chapter three and the effects of the fall, we should let the first two chapters of Genesis sink in. Life was good in the garden. It was a paradise, the ways things were supposed to be. The land was good; creation was good; work was good; marriage was good. There was a perfect innocence to all that God had created. Men and women had nothing to hide. No shame, no embarrassment, no guilt. They were fully upright and fully honorable. And the world was full of perfect relationships: Father, Son and Holy Spirit in constant love and mutual glory; man and nature in cooperation instead of competition; and male and female in a perfectly harmonious and perfectly ordered union of equality and difference.

Genesis 3: Marred by Sin

Unfortunately, the ideal is not always reality. Men and women don't relate to each other as they should. From Genesis 3 onward, the God-given roles for men and women have been perverted. Eve, who was deceived into sin, did so acting independently of man (3:6). And Adam, who sinned no less than his wife, abandoned his responsibilities as a leader. He stood idly by while Eve sinned (3:1-5), followed her into sin (3:6), and then blamed God for giving him Eve in the first place (3:12). Adam failed as a leader. Eve may have been deceived and the first to sin, but Adam, as the leader, was the one who had to give account to God. Adam's sin was not only in disobeying God's command (2:17), but also in throwing off his responsibility as familial head and instead playing the coward and allowing his wife to wear the mantle of leadership (3:17).

So, in the end, both are punished for their disobedience. For man, his unique domain–working the ground–is cursed (3:17). From now on, he will have thorns and thistles to deal with (3:18), and he will live by the sweat of his brow (3:19). For woman, her unique domain–childbearing–is cursed (3:16a). From now on, she will have great pain and anguish in labor, as every mother can attest.

Moreover, God said to the woman, "Your desire shall be for your husband, and he shall rule over you" (3:16b). Man, as the head, should gently and lovingly lead, protect, and provide for his wife. Yet, because of sin, the man either abdicates all responsibility (and watches more football), or his leadership is perverted and becomes a dictatorship–which is why Ephesians 5:25 says "husbands, love." Woman, as the helper, should graciously submit to and support her husband. Yet, because of sin, her submission is perverted and she becomes a usurper–which is why Ephesians 5:22 says "wives, submit."

The word "desire" in Genesis 3:16 does not mean romantic desire, as if God cursed the woman by making her need a man. Rather, the desire is a desire for mastery. This is the same Hebrew word used in Genesis 4:7b, "...sin is crouching at the door. Its desire is for you, but you must rule over it." That the meaning of "desire" in 3:16 is the same as the "desire" in 4:7 is clear from the obvious verbal parallel between the two verses:

3:16b Your desire shall be for your husband, and he shall rule over you.

w'el–ishek tishuqatek wehu yimshal–bak

4:7b Its desire is for you, but you must rule over it.

w'elek teshuqatu w'atah timshal–bo

Just as sin desired to have mastery over Cain, so the woman, tainted by sin, desires to have mastery over her husband (EN 5).

But this is not the way it's supposed to be. God did not make domineering wives and doormat-or-dictator husbands; sin did. God's design has always been mutual love working itself out in male headship and female submission.

CHAPTER FOUR

JESUS AND THE
GOSPELS

Jesus Honored Women

Out of a cultural background that minimized the dignity of women and even depersonalized them, Jesus boldly affirmed their worth and gladly benefitted from their vital ministry. Jesus made the unusual practice of speaking freely to women, and in public no less (John 4:27; 8:10-11; Luke 7:12-13). He also frequently ministered to the needs of hurting women, like Peter's mother-in-law (Mark 1:30-31), the woman bent over for eighteen years (Luke 13:10-17), the bleeding woman (Matt. 9:20-22), and the Syrophoenician woman (Mark 7:24-30).

Jesus not only ministered to women, he allowed women to minister to him. Women anointed Jesus and he warmly received their service (Luke 7:36-50; Matt. 26:6-13). Some women helped Jesus' ministry financially (Luke 8:2-3), while others offered hospitality (Luke 10:40; John 12:2). A number of women–Mary Magdalene, Joanna, Susanna, Mary the mother of James and Joses, Salome, Mary and Martha–are mentioned by name in the gospels, indicating their important place in Jesus' ministry. Many women were among Jesus' band of disciples. And perhaps most significantly, women were the first witnesses to the resurrection (Matt. 28:5-8; Mark 16:1-8; Luke 24:2-9; John 20:1-2).

Underlying Jesus' ministry was the radical assumption that women had value and purpose. The clearest example is his mother Mary, who is called highly favored in Luke 1:28. Moreover, Jesus used women as illustrations in his teaching, mentioning the queen of the south (Matt. 12:42), the widow of Zarephath (Luke 4:26), women at the second coming (Matt. 24:41), and the woman in search of her lost coin (Luke 15:8-10). He held up the persistent widow as an example of prayerfulness (Luke 18:1-5), and the poor widow's offering as an example of generosity (Luke 21:1-4). Jesus addressed women tenderly as "daughters of Abraham," placing them on the same spiritual plane as men (Luke 13:16). Jesus' teaching on divorce treated women as persons, not mere property (Matt. 5:32; 19:9), and his instruction about lust protected women from being treated as nothing more than objects of sexual desire (Matt. 5:28). And in a time where female learning was suspect, Jesus made a point to teach women on numerous occasions (Luke 10:38-42; 23:27-31; John 11:20ff).

Jesus Chose Men for Leadership

Jesus' revolutionary treatment of women was, nevertheless, consistent with God's original design for role distinctions. The most obvious example is Jesus' selection of an all-male apostolic leadership. Granted, that Jesus chose only men to be apostles does not prove conclusively he was a "complementarian," but it does indicate that his revolutionary attitude toward women stopped short of including them in all forms of leadership. And it won't do to say that Jesus was simply going along with the social customs of the day. Jesus had no problem breaking social taboos, which is why he mingled with tax collectors, ate without washing his hands, redefined the Sabbath, reinterpreted the Temple, condemned the Pharisees, and even honored women! The fact is that while he overturned some Jewish interpretations (e.g., about divorce, lust, retribution, etc.), Jesus never rejected biblical teaching from the Old Testament (Matt. 5:17). Jesus honored women in a counter-cultural way without rejecting everything he inherited from his Jewish-Old Testament background concerning men and women.

Further, that Jesus called only Jewish males as apostles does not mean that for Jesus to be making a statement about normative male leadership he must also be making a statement about normative Jewish leadership. The Jewishness of the apostles is linked to a particular moment in salvation history, while their maleness is not. After Pentecost, the kingdom Jesus ushered was no longer for the Jews alone.

Gentiles like Luke and Titus assumed positions of teaching and leadership. But when the disciples needed a successor to Judas, the apostles looked for a *man* who had been with them (Acts 1:21-22).

In summary, Jesus honored women and empowered them for ministry, but when it came to selecting those for positions of leadership and authority, he chose only men.

1 CORINTHIANS 11:2-16

²Now I commend you because you remember me in everything and maintain the traditions even as I delivered them to you. ³But I want you to understand that the head of every man is Christ, the head of a wife is her husband, and the head of Christ is God. ⁴Every man who prays or prophesies with his head covered dishonors his head, ⁵but every wife who prays or prophesies with her head uncovered dishonors her head—it is the same as if her head were shaven. ⁶For if a wife will not cover her head, then she should cut her hair short. But since it is disgraceful for a wife to cut off her hair or shave her head, let her cover her head. ⁷For a man ought not to cover his head, since he is the image and glory of God, but woman is the glory of man. ⁸For man was not made from woman, but woman from man. ⁹Neither was man created for woman, but woman

for man. [10]That is why a wife ought to have a symbol of authority on her head, because of the angels. [11]Nevertheless, in the Lord woman is not independent of man nor man of woman; [12]for as woman was made from man, so man is now born of woman. And all things are from God. [13]Judge for yourselves: is it proper for a wife to pray to God with her head uncovered? [14]Does not nature itself teach you that if a man wears long hair it is a disgrace for him, [15]but if a woman has long hair, it is her glory? For her hair is given to her for a covering. [16]If anyone is inclined to be contentious, we have no such practice, nor do the churches of God.

The following three chapters deal with the three main passages concerning the roles of men and women in the church. In the first of these three chapters, rather than giving a verse by verse commentary on 1 Corinthians 11:2-16, I will simply highlight some observations that pertain to manhood and womanhood.

Observation 1: The husband is the head of his wife

Verse 3 outlines a series of overlapping relationships. "The head of every man is Christ, the head of a wife is her husband, and the head of Christ is God." Anyone familiar with the scholarship on this issue knows that the little word "head" (*kephale*) has killed a lot of trees. Scholars, using their expertise in Greek and the latest computer software, have gone back and forth in articles and books arguing whether *kephale* means "authority over" or "source" (like the head of a river is its source). I happen to think that the evidence points squarely in the direction of "authority over" (EN 6), but even if "source" is sometimes the meaning of *kephale*, as egalitarians suggest, I don't see how a traditional understanding of male headship is thereby nullified. We know from other passages that wives are to submit to their husbands and respect them like Sarah respected Abraham when she called him "lord" (Eph. 5:22, 33; 1 Peter 3:1-6), so how can we avoid connotations of authority in the marriage relationship even if *kephale* were to mean source?

Besides, we have incontrovertible examples in Paul's writings where *kephale* must mean something like "authority over." In Ephesians 1, Paul says that Christ has been seated at God's right hand in the heavenly places, far above all *rule* and *authority* and *power* and *dominion,* and all things have been placed under his feet and he has been made head (*kephale*) over all things to the church (1:20-22). The context demands that *kephale* refer to Christ's authority over the church, not merely that the church has its origin in Christ. Likewise, in Ephesians 5, Paul says wives are to submit to their husbands, for the husband is the head of the wife even as Christ is the head of the church (5:22-23). Citing the headship of the husband as a reason for the wife's submission makes little sense if headship implies only source or origin without any reference to male leadership. *Kephale,* in at least these two instances in Ephesians, must mean "authority over." And there are no grammatical or contextual reasons to think that Paul is using *kephale* in a different way in 1 Corinthians 11.

Therefore, we should understand verse 3 as saying that Christ has authority over mankind; the husband has authority over his wife (the Greek words for man and woman are the same for husband and wife); and God has authority over Christ (that is, God the Son submits to God the Father). Thus, we have two spiritually equal creatures (man and woman) with two different, but complementary roles. The woman is the helper and support of the man, while the man is the head of the woman. The roles are not status symbols or value markers; they are simply different roles.

This hits upon perhaps the main disagreement in the whole debate. Egalitarians believe emphatically that equality and subordination (their word for male headship and role distinctions) are inherently contradictory. They believe that subordination is the same as denigration, and equality the same as indistinguishability (when it comes to roles).

Complementarians disagree. Within the Godhead we see the opposite dynamic: subordination without denigration and equality with distinct roles. The Spirit, equal in worth, honor, and dignity with the Father and the Son, does not speak on his own authority, but ministers what he hears so that Jesus Christ might be glorified (John 16:13-15). The Son, equal in worth, honor, and dignity with God, did nothing of his own authority, but only spoke what his Father told him (John 8:28). In his final hours, the confession of the perfect and submissive Son of God was "not my will, but yours, be done" (Luke 22:42). As Paul puts it, God is the head of Christ (1 Cor. 11:3).

The Father and the Son share the same essence and rank, and yet in their relationship, the Son submits to the Father while the Father never submits to the Son. No inferiority. No inequality. Yet, different roles. Granted, complementarians sometimes speak too quickly about the "eternal subordination of the Son." It is better to say that there has always been an "order" (*taxis*) in the Trinity–an order not of rank, but of well-arranged relationships. The Father sends the Son, and the Father and the Son send the Spirit, and the relations are not reversible. Mutuality and equality exist in the Trinity alongside a divinely instituted order. Calvin writes, "For even though we admit that *in respect to order and degree the beginning of divinity is in the Father,* yet we say that it is a detestable invention that essence [being] is proper to the Father alone, as if he were the deifer of the Son" (EN 7). With the Trinity as our model, then, we understand that authority and God-given order in the church, or, headship and submission in marriage, are not inconsistent with equality of personhood.

Observation 2: Men and women are interdependent.

In order to clarify any potential misunderstanding about the value of women compared to men, Paul stresses that although they have different roles, men and women are dependent upon each other (1 Cor. 11:11-12). Woman came from man (his rib) and was created for him (and not the other way around), but, subsequently, men come from women (through childbirth). Neither man nor woman is independent of the other. The only truly independent being is God, from whom and through whom come all things (11:12).

Observation 3: Women can speak in church

If 1 Corinthians 11 details instructions for corporate worship–and I think it does (notice the material to follow concerning the Lord's Supper and spiritual gifts in the assembly)–then we can say without a doubt that women are allowed to speak in church. Paul assumed that women would pray and prophesy (11:5). Services at Corinth were probably less structured than ours tend to be and women as well as men were able to give a spontaneous prayer, a song, a tongue, or a word of prophecy (for more on prophecy as distinct from preaching see the next chapter on 1 Corinthians 14). In short, women could, and did, speak in the church. Churches today which prohibit women from singing (because songs can teach), or praying (because it might be exhortative), or even giving announcements (because it's speaking period) pull in the boundaries for participation in worship closer than the Bible demands.

Observation 4: Women in Corinth were to wear head coverings. Women today are not required to wear head coverings, but they must show respect for gender distinctions.

This will take some explaining. There are a least four interpretative issues that need to be settled before we can reach this conclusion.

What is the covering? Some argue that the head covering is long hair. After all, doesn't verse 15 (NIV) tell us "long hair is given to her as a covering"? Long hair, though, is probably not the covering for a couple of reasons. First, verse 15 does not have to mean that long hair is given *instead* of a covering, it can mean simply, that hair is given *as* a covering. The argument from verse 14 into 15 suggests that long hair is not the covering required in worship, but is indicative of the fact that a covering is required (see also verse 6 where an uncovered head is not identical to, but is as disgraceful as, a shaved head). Second, the covering was not for all of life or even all of corporate worship; it was only necessary for women when praying or prophesying. Because the covering is only required in specific occasions, hair, which goes with a woman everywhere, cannot be the covering.

So what was the covering? One educated guess is that it was some type of shawl. More than likely, it was not a veil as we see in certain Muslim countries, because face coverings were not common in Greek culture. No one knows for sure, but the covering in question was possibly a small wrap-around scarf-like garment that could be placed on the head when praying and prophesying.

What "head" does the woman dishonor (verse 5)? One of the difficulties in this section is that the word "head" is used throughout the passage with different, sometimes multiple, meanings. Thus, "man who prays or prophesies with his head covered dishonors his head" means that every man who covers his physical head dishonors his spiritual head, that is Christ (verses 3,4). So what about the woman? She too dishonors her head when her (physical) head is uncovered. The "head" she dishonors is Christ, but also her husband. The wife's actions reflect on her husband, because she is his glory (verse 7, cf. Prov. 31:23). So when the rebellious wife goes uncovered, her actions dishonor both God and the husband whose headship she is rejecting.

What does Paul mean by "authority" (verse 10)? Paul may be saying that the woman must wear a covering as a sign that she is under the husband's authority (although the word "sign" is not in the Greek). But "authority" is never used in this passive sense; it is always active. Therefore, instead of taking "authority" to mean the authority over the woman, we should understand the "authority" on the woman's head to be her own. That is, when she is properly covered, the woman has the authority (the right) to pray and prophesy. The "sign" of authority on her head is the authority she has to participate in worship as a long as she demonstrates true femininity and does not reject her husband's headship.

What does Paul mean by "the very nature of things" (verse 14)? Does nature refer to the prevailing customs of the day? Doubtful. Nature, in Paul's mind, seems to be more than majority opinion. For people sometimes "do by nature things required by the law" (Romans 2:14 NIV). There is something transcultural in Paul's use of the word (see Romans 1:26 where Paul disparages homosexuality as contrary to nature). He uses nature as an appeal to the God-given sense of decency and propriety which remains even in our fallen world.

Does nature, then, teach us that women should have long hair and men's hair should be short? Not exactly. Men can grow as much hair as women (and sometimes do). More importantly, the Bible does not always outlaw long hair for men. You may recall that Samson was told not to cut his hair as part of a Nazirite vow (Judg. 13:5; Num. 6:1ff).

So what is Paul getting at? There is a curious mix (at least it seems curious to those of us twenty centuries removed from the original audience) of nature and first century custom in Paul's argument. Nature doesn't teach us how long our hair should be. Culture teaches us what are acceptable hair lengths for men and women. Nature, though, teaches us that men ought to adorn themselves like men and women like women. The natural God-given inclination of men and women is to be ashamed of that which confuses their gender. Culture gives us the symbols of masculinity and femininity, while nature dictates that men should embrace their manhood, and women embrace their womanhood.

So, back to the main issue at hand. Should women still cover their heads while praying and prophesying? Probably not. First, because it is impossible to know precisely what the head coverings were like. Being largely ignorant of the practice, any attempt at exact obedience would be more symbolic than actual.

Second, although Paul appeals to the created order in this passage, he stops short of explicitly grounding head coverings in God's original design. Because of the created order of the sexes, according to verse 10, the woman ought to have a sign of authority on her head. But notice, Paul doesn't give specific details as to the type of covering the woman should wear. Clearly, he has in mind a head covering for the Corinthians, but what the creation order supports is not a certain kind of shawl, but a symbol of authority. That's the key. When women pray and prophesy in the assembly, they must do so with some sign that signifies their authority to do so. In other words, something must tell the congregation, "This women speaking in public is not throwing off her role as the glory of man. She is still in submission to her husband (if she has one), and therefore has authority to speak."

No one knows for sure what the covering was like or what exactly it pointed to. But everyone recognizes that the covering symbolized something else, be it the authority to prophesy, submission to her husband, married status, femininity or some combination of all of the above. A head covering, in America today, conveys none of these things. If we see a woman in church wearing a hat or shawl or veil we do not think, "Ah-ahh, she's married," or "she's submissive" or "she's a woman." But where culture dictates symbols that do indicate these things, we should not throw them off, literally or figuratively.

Third, Paul's appeal to nature in verse 14 makes difficult an overly-precise application of his foregoing principles. As has been argued, "the nature of things" teaches that long hair, as a cultural expression of femininity, is inappropriate for men. Nature does not instruct us on hair length, but is does teach us that in a culture where it is a symbol of femininity, long hair should be a disgrace to men. Nature teaches us that a woman should accept her role as a woman, but the expression of womanhood will be somewhat culturally conditioned. I know this is all a bit vague, and some of us would like some hard and fast rules about hair length, but in this instance we are forced to live with some ambiguity. We can assert, without equivocation, that God wants men to look like men and women to look like women, but what that physically looks like will vary from time to time and place to place.

As I said earlier, reading the Bible as the word of God does not require that we try to re-create the first century. We must separate principle from practice.

The principle rooted in the created order is that of gender distinctions, in particular, male headship and female submission. The practice stipulated is that men and women participating in public worship do so in a way that demonstrates this principle. In twenty-first century North American culture, for example, men shouldn't wear dresses, and woman probably shouldn't cut their hair just like men. Likewise, women in this culture, with some exceptions, should probably take their husband's last name, as a sign of his headship (EN 8). Women may not have to wear head coverings, but they should demonstrate submission to their husbands and show proper expressions of femininity.

One final note. Verse 16 is sometimes used to disavow verses 2-15. The NIV reads, "If anyone wants to be contentious about this, we have no other practice–nor do the churches of God." This translation makes perfect sense, in effect saying: "If anyone disagrees about head coverings, you shouldn't, because it is practiced in all the churches." Some translations (like the ESV), however, translate the phrase as "we have no *such* practice." This makes it sound like Paul is dismissing his whole argument, which surely is not his point. The Greek word *toioutos* can mean "such" or "other." If it is "such," we should understand Paul saying, "we have no such practice of being contentious," not "we have no such practice of wearing head coverings."

CHAPTER SIX

1 CORINTHIANS 14:26-40

As in all the churches of the saints, [34]the women should keep silent in the churches. For they are not permitted to speak, but should be in submission, as the Law also says. [35]If there is anything they desire to learn, let them ask their husbands at home. For it is shameful for a woman to speak in church.

There are numerous interpretative issues that plague this text. Thankfully, only one is our concern, and that surrounds verses 33b-35:

The big question is: How can Paul command women to be silent in the churches in chapter 14 when he regulates women praying and prophesying in chapter 11? Do women pray and prophesy in church, or are they to be silent?

Some have resolved this dilemma by writing off Paul as hopelessly contradictory. Others treat 1 Corinthians 11 as hypothetical instructions—how women should adorn themselves if they *could* pray and prophesy, which, of course, they can't. Still others see Paul as dealing with different contexts in the two chapters—1 Corinthians 11 dealing with informal gatherings where women may speak and 1 Corinthians 14 dealing with more formal church assemblies where women must be silent. And yet others imagine Paul is simply exaggerating in 1 Corinthians 14 because he has "had it up to here" with the noisy Corinthian women.

Let me suggest another alternative, one that is not at all unique to me: Paul allowed women to prophesy, but did not allow them to join in the weighing of prophecy.

If we are going to make sense of this passage we need to understand the difference between prophesying and teaching. The nature of New Testament prophecy is not identical to Old Testament prophecy. Old Testament prophecy was absolutely authoritative, while in the New Testament era, the gift of prophecy must be weighed and sifted (1 Thess. 5:20-21; 1 Cor. 14:29). Consequently, prophecy on this side of Pentecost is not an exercise of authoritative instruction. Rather, it is a Spirit-prompted revelation that must be tested against accepted teaching. It was not prophecy, but apostolic teaching, that formed the ethical and theological bedrock of the early church. Thus, elders do not need the gift of prophecy, but they must be able to teach (1 Tim. 3:2). Likewise, the first pastors may or may not have been prophets, but they certainly were teachers (1 Tim. 4:11; 5:17; 6:2; 2 Tim. 2:2; Titus 1:9; 2:1ff). Teaching–the explanation and application of Scripture–is authoritative instruction in a way that prophecy is not. With this understanding of prophecy, it seems reasonable that women could prophesy in the church, but could not teach men (1 Tim. 2:11-12).

Still, with women prophesying and praying at Corinth, how are we to understand Paul's command for silence in 1 Corinthians 14? The answer lies in verse 29: "Let two or three prophets speak, and let the others weigh what is said." If the command for "silence" in verses 33-35 refers to the first half of verse 29, Paul flatly contradicts himself within the space of four chapters. He tells women to prophesy with their heads covered in chapter 11 and then orders them to refrain from prophesying in chapter 14. But if "silence" refers to the second half of verse 29, Paul's injunction looks more plausible. Instead of forbidding women from speaking altogether, he prohibits them from weighing prophecy. Thus, verses 26-28 regulate prophetic speech; verses 30-35 regulate the weighing and sifting of prophetic speech; and verse 29 is the transition verse that joins the two sets of regulative instructions.

All that to say, the command for women to be silent must be understood in context. Just as the command for the tongue-speaker to keep silent does not forbid him from ever saying anything in church (14:28), so the command for women to be silent does not assume that in all situations women cannot speak. The explicit situation in which women must be silent is where prophecies are being evaluated. Such evaluation would have involved teaching and the exercise of authority (over other prophets), two activities Paul consistently denies to women. If women have questions regarding the weighing of prophecies, they should ask their husbands at home, lest they violate the principle of submission and disgrace themselves (14:34-35).

In the end, 1 Corinthians 11 and 14 fit together nicely. Women are encouraged to participate in worship of the gathered assembly, but their participation must avoid authoritative teaching over men.

CHAPTER SEVEN

1 TIMOTHY 2:8-15

[8]I desire then that in every place the men should pray, lifting holy hands without anger or quarreling; [9]likewise also that women should adorn themselves in respectable apparel, with modesty and self-control, not with braided hair and gold or pearls or costly attire, [10]but with what is proper for women who profess godliness—with good works. [11]Let a woman learn quietly with all submissiveness. [12]I do not permit a woman to teach or to exercise authority over a man; rather, she is to remain quiet. [13]For Adam was formed first, then Eve; [14]and Adam was not deceived, but the woman was deceived and became a transgressor. [15]Yet she will be saved through childbearing—if they continue in faith and love and holiness, with self-control.

Because this third section from 1 Timothy is in many ways the heart of the matter, and literally almost every word is in dispute, I will move more methodically through this passage, giving a verse by verse exposition.

Context

Timothy was a leader, perhaps what we might today call a pastor, in the church at Ephesus. Timothy's location is thought by some to be highly significant. For many claim that Ephesus was a hotbed for radical feminism, that the cult of the goddess Artemis typified the "feminist principle" that saturated first century Ephesus. With this as the perceived background, it is then argued that 1 Timothy is highly unique and its commands limited to the extreme feminism rampant in the immediate culture.

The problem with this reconstruction is that it is more fiction than fact. Ephesus was a fairly typical Greco-Roman city (EN 9). The political, cultural, and religious elements were not out of the ordinary. Like other ancient cities, the magistrates of Ephesus were male. Likewise, the civic groups in Ephesus were dominated by men. The religious climate was, not surprisingly, polytheistic. Temples and houses throughout the city boasted any number of gods and goddesses. And even though priestesses were common in Greek cities, most of the deities in Ephesus were served by priests. True, Ephesus was famous as the city of the goddess Artemis (Acts 19:35), and no doubt women participated in the cultic rituals along with men. But the description of Artemis of the Ephesians in Acts 19 tells us nothing that would make us think there was a proto-feminist ethos surrounding Timothy's congregation. In fact, all the main characters mentioned by Luke are men: Demetrius who made silver shrines of Artemis was a man (verse 24); he addressed the crowd as "men" (verse 25, cf. verse 35); the Asiarchs (NIV has "officials of the province") would have been men (verse 31); and the city clerk would have been a man as well (verse 35). Of course, one must be careful not to read too much into a narrative account like Acts 19 that has nothing to do with gender roles in the church. But that's precisely my point. We should be leery of scholars making sweeping statements about life in Ephesus (or anywhere else) based on a reconstruction of first century texts and inscriptions that can only be described as creative at best. Contrary to some scholarly imagination (which has proved to be more imagination than scholarship [EN 10]), the Bible's depiction of Ephesus gives no indication that men were not in charge of the resources and religious activities in the temple of Artemis, as they were in the religious centers all throughout the ancient world.

Ephesus simply was not a radically feminist place. Some of the privileged girls of the city were, in fact, praised for their modesty and devotion to their husbands, clearly not the kinds of virtues that reign in a feminist stronghold. The roles–both good and bad–that women filled in Ephesus were no different than the roles women filled in other ancient cities: wives, mothers, farmers, home-managers, bar-girls, prostitutes, and fortune-tellers. This is not to suggest that Ephesus was especially harsh toward women. It is only to say, that in terms of gender roles, first century Ephesus was unremarkable.

Besides, whatever Ephesus was like, we should not think that Paul's focus in 1 Timothy is especially narrow. He writes so that "you will know how people ought to conduct themselves in God's household, which is the church of the living God" (1 Tim. 3:15 NIV). To be sure, every piece of writing is conditioned by its recipients. Yet, while Paul addresses specific problems (as he does in all his letters), he never suggests that the principles set forth are culturally limited. Rather, as 1 Timothy 3:15 indicates, Paul is concerned more broadly with how believers conduct themselves in God's household, wherever it may be.

Verse 8 "I desire then that in every place the men should pray, lifting holy hands without anger or quarreling."

Paul begins this section on worship instructions by addressing men. The men are to lift up their hands in prayer. The emphasis, though, is not on posture. Prayer in the Bible is sometimes standing, sometimes kneeling, sometimes lying prostrate (1 Kings 8:54; Psalm 95:6; Dan. 6:10; Matt. 26:39; Luke 22:41; Acts 9:40; Rev. 11:16). Posture is not the point; piety is. Men should pray with *holy* hands, *without anger or quarreling.* Paul's instructions move inward, from appearance in prayer to attitude in prayer.

Verses 9-10 "likewise also that women should adorn themselves in respectable apparel, with modesty and self-control, not with braided hair and gold or pearls or costly attire, but with what is proper for women who profess godliness–with good works."

Paul now shifts his focus and addresses the women. He commands women to dress respectably and then adds three clarifying clauses. First, women are to dress with modesty and self-control. There should be a sense of propriety, moderation, and a refraining from sensuality. Second, women are to dress not with braided hair or gold or pearls or expensive clothes. Such items flaunted wealth and drew attention to external beauty rather than "the unfading beauty of a gentle and quiet spirit" (1 Peter 3:3-4 NIV). Third, women are to dress with good works. As with the men, Paul moves inward, from appearance to attitude. His main concern is that women adorn themselves in a manner fitting the gospel.

These two verses are often used to negate whatever else Paul commands of women, because if braided hair is cultural, so the argument goes, then the other commands for women must be as well. But the prohibition of braided hair and the like is far from Paul's main point. It only clarifies how women are to dress modestly. His focus is on internal maturity and its accompanying external modesty. Braided hair, gold, pearls and expensive clothes are not intrinsic evils. Heaven is full of gold and pearls (Rev. 21:18-21), and the Old Testament priestly garments were expensive and ornate (Ex. 28). The problem with these items is their abuse.

This is confirmed by a parallel passage in 1 Peter 3:3-4. There, women are commanded, "Do not let your adorning be external—the braiding of hair, the wearing of gold, *or the putting on of clothing*—but let your adorning be the hidden person of the heart" (emphasis added). Literally, Peter did not condemn a certain kind of clothing, just clothing itself. Yet clearly, women do not have to go to church without any clothes whatsoever. Dress is not the fundamental problem, even though that's literally what Peter mentions. The issue arises when the putting on of clothes (or the wearing of pearls and gold and braids) becomes immodest. Peter's concern, like Paul's in 1 Timothy, is that women labor to make themselves beautiful on the inside, not on the outside.

Verse 11 "Let a woman learn quietly with all submissiveness."

It is worth noting that Paul is stepping out of mainstream Judaism by commanding women to learn. Some segments of Judaism considered it downright sinful for women to learn the Scriptures. Paul disagreed. He was eager for women to learn, provided they did so "in quietness and full submission" (NIV).

"Quietness" or "silence" (verse 12) is not meant to be demeaning. They are positive qualities for the learner (see Eccl. 9:17). And as we've seen from 1 Corinthians 11 and 14, silence is not an absolute command encompassing every element of corporate worship. Silence, in this text as well as 1 Corinthians 14, refers to the teaching ministry of the church. In the context of corporate worship, women are not to be teachers, but quiet learners.

"All submissiveness" clarifies why women are expected to be quiet. They are to be submissive to men, specifically a wife to her husband (Eph. 5:22; Col. 3:18; Titus 2:5; 1 Peter 3:1). In short, a woman who learns quietly embraces her submissive role and honors God's design for the sexes.

Verse 12 "I do not permit a woman to teach or to exercise authority over a man; rather, she is to remain quiet."

Verses 11 and 12 form a single unit. The central idea–women should be silent–bookends the unit. Thus, the command for quietness and submission begins verse 11 and the command for silence finishes verse 12. In the middle, we have an explanation of what it means for women to learn in quietness and full submission. Women should not teach (respecting the command for quietness) and should not have authority over a man (respecting the command for all submissiveness).

"I do not permit" Some argue that since the verb "permit" (*epitrepo*) is in the present tense we should really understand Paul as saying, "I am not presently allowing a woman to teach," the implication being, "but I may allow a woman to teach at another time." But this is an unreasonable understanding of grammar. If present tense verbs only carry weight for the time in which they were written, much of the New Testament has no significance for us whatsoever. In the Pastoral Epistles alone (1 Timothy, 2 Timothy, Titus), there are 111 present tense verbs like "permit" here in verse 12. If these verbs do not extend beyond Paul's initial audience, then God no longer "desires all people to be saved" (1 Tim. 2:4), the "mystery of godliness" is no longer great (1 Tim. 3:16), and there is no "great gain in godliness with contentment" (1 Tim. 6:6).

"a woman to teach" Paul is not specific about what a woman may not teach. Perhaps he is only commanding women to avoid teaching error (she was unlearned, right?), but other kinds of teaching are permissible. This reasoning sounds attractive, but will not work. First, the verse doesn't say anything about teaching error or woman being unlearned; it simply says, "I do not permit a woman to teach." Besides, how ignorant could the Ephesian women be if Paul taught among them day and night for three years? (Acts 20:31) Second, Paul does not use the word for false teaching (*heterodidaskaleo*) like he does in 1 Timothy 1:3 and 6:3. He uses the word "teaching" (*didaskein*). Except in Titus 1:11 where the context absolutely demands false teaching, *didaskein* in the Pastoral Epistles is used in a positive sense of teaching the truth of the gospel or the apostolic message (see 1 Tim. 4:11; 6:2; 2 Tim. 2:2). Third, why would Paul prohibit women, but not men, from teaching error, especially when the false teachers mentioned by name in the Pastoral Epistles are all men (Phygelus, Hermogenes, Hymenaeus, Philetus, Demas, and Alexander the metalworker).

"or to exercise authority over a man" Again, there is considerable debate over the meaning of the word "authority" (*authentein*, which is the infinitive form of the verb *authenteo*). Some scholars suggest that *authentein* should be translated "to domineer" which is the sense one gets from the King James Version: "to usurp authority." If *authentein* means "to domineer," then Paul may not be prohibiting women from having authority, but simply from getting it improperly. This would change the meaning of the text significantly.

A more likely translation, however, is simply "authority" (as per the NIV, NASB, NLT, ESV, RSV, and NRSV). This is the best translation based on the following considerations:

First, it would be strange for Paul to warn women against domineering, but not men, given that he is writing to a man and the false teachers we know of were men (see the list above).

Second, teaching and authority are so closely linked in this verse that both must be either positive or negative. The phrase "I do not permit a woman to teach or to exercise authority" is, to put it syntactically, a negated finite verb + infinitive + *oude* ("nor" in Greek) + infinitive. Recent studies have discovered this exact pattern forty-nine times in extra biblical sources, not to mention at least once in the New Testament in Acts 16:21. In every case the infinitive verbs are either both positive or both negative (EN 11). So Paul is either forbidding women from teaching error and domineering, or he is forbidding them from teaching and having authority over men altogether. The latter seems to be the case because (1) *didaskein* is almost always used positively in the Pastoral Episitles; (2) there is no object after *didaskein* (like "error" or "falsehood"); and (3) verses 13-14 which give Paul's reasons for the command (verse 13 especially) would be unnecessary if he were only forbidding teaching error and domineering.

Third, where *authenteo* is used outside of the New Testament (it's only used in the New Testament in this verse), it does not mean "to domineer" or "usurp authority." It can mean to rule, to control, to act independently, or to be responsible, but it does not carry the negative sense "to usurp" or "domineer." The word is used in different ways, but the unifying concept is that of authority (EN 12).

In the end, the best overall option is to see "no teaching" and "no authority over a man" as the explanation of what it means for a woman to learn in quietness (without teaching) and full submission (without authority over men). Thus, verse 12 could be summarized: "God desires women to be silent and submissive in the church, which means that women should not be public teachers over men nor exercise authority over men."

Verses 13-14 "For Adam was formed first, then Eve; and Adam was not deceived, but the woman was deceived and became a transgressor."

After stating the principle ("Let a woman learn quietly with all submissiveness") and further explaining it ("I do not permit a woman to teach or to exercise authority over a man"), Paul now backs up his argument with two reasons.

The word "for" (*gar*) tips us off that Paul is now giving us his reasons for verses 11 and 12. In the New Testament, *gar* most often expresses cause or reason. Thirty-three times it is used in the Pastoral Epistles; thirty times expressing cause. Despite this fact, some scholars prefer to see "for" in verse 13 as illustrative rather than causal. That is, they understand Paul to be giving an illustration of his principle instead of giving reasons for it. To be fair, it is grammatically possible that Paul's use of "for" in verse 13 is only illustrative, but the fact that Paul is issuing a command (given negatively as "I do not permit"), makes such a use highly unlikely. Nine times in his letters Paul gives an imperative command followed with *gar*; and in every instance *gar* functions in a causal sense. In the Pastoral Epistles, Paul issues a command or a command-idea (like "I do not permit") followed by *gar* 21 times, all of which require the causal sense. It is best, therefore, to keep the normal sense of *gar* and see "for" in verse 13 as introducing Paul's reasons for verses 11 and 12.

Reason #1: Order of Creation (verse 13) The first reason why women are not to teach or have authority is based on the order of creation. Adam was formed first, then Eve. Some object, "What about animals then? They were created before Adam so why don't they have priority?" But this misses Paul's point. He is not making a definitive statement that applies to every bit of the sequence of creation. His thinking is perfectly consistent with the Old Testament idea of the first-born. The first-born was accorded special rights because he was the first born son in the family, regardless of whether animals had been born in the household or not. The issue of other creatures was as irrelevant for primogeniture as it to Paul's argument here.

Reason #2: Eve was deceived (verse 14) This can be interpreted in one of two ways. Paul may be making a statement about the nature of women; namely, that they are more easily deceived than men. This understanding does not say that women are inferior to men or less capable of piety than men. Rather, according to this interpretation, women and men have different inclinations which render them liable to different temptations. Men, who are generally more calculating, may be on the whole more particularly tempted to harshness or schism. Women, who are generally more relational than men, may be on the whole more particularly tempted to doctrinal deception because of their tendency to prize harmonious relationships more than men. If Eve's deception speaks to the nature of women, then Paul forbids teaching or authority because women–who outshine men in other areas–are on the whole more easily deceived.

There is, however, another understanding of verse 14. Paul may be making a statement about what happens when the roles of men and women are reversed. Adam was supposed to be the head, responsible for loving leadership and direction. But he abdicated his role and Eve took on the mantle of leadership instead. As a result of this role-reversal, sin entered into the world. On this understanding, Paul is pointing to the difference between the two guilty persons: Adam sinned openly, but Eve was deceived. In highlighting this difference, Paul may be grounding his argument in God's design for men and women, which was tragically supplanted in the Fall.

No matter our understanding of verse 14, it should be obvious that Paul does not ground the silence and submission of women in first century culture. In fact, he does precisely the opposite. His rationale for role distinctions in the church harkens back to Genesis. Paul does not permit a woman to teach or exercise authority over a man because to do so would be a violation of God's original design for the sexes in the created order, where the man was given headship and the woman was given to be his helpmate.

Verse 15 "Yet she will be saved through childbearing–if they continue in faith and love and holiness, with self-control."

This difficult verse is usually understood in one of two ways. Some see verse 15 as a reference to Mary. Through the Virgin Birth, the Messiah entered the world and subsequently women (and men) were saved. This interpretation is plausible. Paul, having already alluded to the opening chapters of Genesis, could be thinking of Genesis 3:15 which prophesied that the seed of the woman would crush Satan. If so, the definite article ("the") before childbearing (in the Greek but not in most English translations) would be emphasized. Women are not saved through childbearing, but through *the* childbirth, the birth of Jesus.

There is a second common interpretation, one that, in my opinion, has more merit. If we understand that "salvation" in the New Testament does not necessarily mean justification, we can make more sense of the verse. Most of us read "salvation" and think of giving our lives to Christ and "getting saved." But salvation has a much broader scope in the New Testament, covering the entire life of the Christian, not just a single definitive moment of faith and repentance. Elsewhere, we are commanded to work out our salvation with fear and trembling (Phil. 2:12), not as meriting favor with God, but as a striving for Christian obedience. This is the sense of salvation Paul has in mind when he says that women will be saved through childbearing.

Giving birth is one of the ways in which a woman demonstrates obedience to her God-given identity. Instead of casting off all order and decency, a godly woman embraces her true femininity in dressing modestly, learning quietly, bearing children, and continuing in faith, love and holiness. Understandably, some women will not have children because of medical reasons or singleness, but in so far as it is possible, childbearing is one of the unique ways in which a women can accept, in obedience, her God-given role.

In these eight controversial verses (1 Tim. 2:8-15) we see how manhood and womanhood work out in the church. Just as in the home, husbands should love their wives and not be harsh with them (Col. 3:19), so in the church, men should lift holy hands in prayer, without anger or disputing (1 Tim. 2:8). And just as wives are submissive to their husbands in the home (Col. 3:18), so in God's household women ought to learn in quietness and full submission, refraining from teaching or having authority over men (1 Tim. 2:11-12). Rather, as women embrace God's design, adorning themselves with modesty and conducting themselves with propriety, they will be working out their salvation, even as God works in them "both to will and to work for his good pleasure" (Phil. 2:13).

CHAPTER EIGHT

1 TIMOTHY 3:1-13

[1]The saying is trustworthy: If anyone aspires to the office of overseer, he desires a noble task. [2]Therefore an overseer must be above reproach, the husband of one wife, sober-minded, self-controlled, respectable, hospitable, able to teach, [3]not a drunkard, not violent but gentle, not quarrelsome, not a lover of money. [4]He must manage his own household well, with all dignity keeping his children submissive, [5]for if someone does not know how to manage his own household, how will he care for God's church? [6]He must not be a recent convert, or he may become puffed up with conceit and fall into the condemnation of the devil. [7]Moreover, he must be well thought of by outsiders, so that he may not fall into disgrace, into a snare of the devil. [8]Deacons likewise must be dignified, not double-tongued, not addicted to much wine, not greedy for dishonest gain.

⁹They must hold the mystery of the faith with a clear conscience. ¹⁰And let them also be tested first; then let them serve as deacons if they prove themselves blameless. ¹¹Their wives likewise must be dignified, not slanderers, but sober-minded, faithful in all things. ¹²Let deacons each be the husband of one wife, managing their children and their own households well. ¹³For those who serve well as deacons gain a good standing for themselves and also great confidence in the faith that is in Christ Jesus.

Paul goes on in 1 Timothy 3 to give the qualifications for overseers and deacons, from which several important observations can be made.

Observation 1: Two Offices, Two Functions

This is probably a good time to take a step back and say a word about church polity (governance) in the early church. The New Testament knows two distinct church offices, given here as overseers (3:1) and deacons (3:8). An earlier mention of these two offices is made in Philippians 1:1. "Paul and Timothy, servants of Christ Jesus, To all the saints in Christ Jesus who are at Philippi, with the overseers and deacons." Already by the late 50s or early 60s AD, the church was sufficiently organized to have the two offices of elder and deacon.

Notice that I am equating the "elder" in 1 Timothy 3 with the "overseer" of Philippians 1. I use the two terms interchangeably because of Acts 20. There are three Greek words used throughout the

New Testament to describe the spiritual leaders in the church, all of which appear in Acts 20. The first word is *episkopos*, sometimes translated "bishop," usually translated "overseer." The second word is *presbyteros*, translated "elder" or "presbyter." The third word is *poimen*, translated "shepherd" or "pastor." These three words—overseer, elder, pastor—refer to the same office. In Acts 20:17, Paul calls for the elders of the church to come to him before he leaves Ephesus. The word for elder in verse 17 is *presbyteros*. Then in Acts 20:28, while Paul is addressing the elders (the *presbyteros*), he commands them to keep watch over the flock (*poimnion*) as overseers (*episkopos*) and to care for, or pastor (*poimen* in its verb form), the church of God. Notice how these spiritual leaders are called, interchangeably, elders, overseers, and pastors. The three words mean the same thing. In the New Testament, we don't see pastors and bishops above them, or elders and pastors above them. We see two offices in the church: overseer-pastor-elder and deacon.

These two offices serve two different functions, as anticipated in Acts 6:1-7. This passage does not mention by name elders or deacons, but remember we are only in Acts 6. The New Testament church as we know it didn't exist until Acts 2 at Pentecost. So the church is not yet at this point organized in terms of office and structure. But what we see here are the beginnings of the two offices of the church and their two main functions.

Here's the situation: the infant church in Jerusalem was growing by leaps and bounds and, almost immediately, there was a controversy. Church members had fallen through the ministry cracks. The Grecian Jews felt like their widows were being overlooked in the daily distribution of food. This was a problem that couldn't be ignored, but the apostles knew they were not the ones to take care of it. They needed to give their attention to prayer and the ministry of the word. So they appointed seven men known to be full of wisdom and the Spirit to tend to the needy widows.

We see a clear distinction: the apostles will be devoted to spiritual food; the Seven will be devoted to physical food. True, the apostles did collect offerings for other churches and the Seven sometimes preached and performed miracles, so we don't want to make the distinction overly rigid. It's not as if the apostles never lifted a finger to help and the Seven never did anything "spiritual," but there was at least a general distinction which carried over into the offices of elder and deacon. Elders feed with spiritual bread. Deacons feed with physical bread. To put the two functions another way: elders carry out the ministry of the word; deacons carry out the ministry of mercy.

Elders, therefore, will be students of the Bible. They will be men of exemplary character. They will be spiritual leaders. An elder must be able to teach (1 Tim. 3:2), something not required of deacons. Teaching does not have to mean lecturing in a classroom or giving a sermon, but it does mean that elders must know the Bible, know theology, be able to discern truth from error, and know how to communicate it to others. Titus 1:9 says about an elder: "He must hold firm to the trustworthy word as taught, so that he may be able to give instruction in sound doctrine and also to rebuke those who contradict it." Elders minister the word. That is their number one priority.

Deacons, on the other hand, will be first and foremost servants. The Greek word *diakonos* means servant. Thus, deacons serve food and water. They distribute charity to and from the congregation. They serve the body in physical ways. Elders provide spiritual bread; deacons offer physical bread. Elders give ministry oversight; deacons provide daily service. Elders minister in word; deacons in deed (EN 13).

Observation #2: Elders Were Men

There are two clues that lead us to think that elders were men and not women. First, an overseer, we are told, must be "the husband of one wife" (3:2). Literally, he must be "a one woman man." Paul isn't requiring marriage as a prerequisite for eldership–he wasn't married, and neither was Jesus–as much as he is requiring faithfulness. Paul assumes that an elder will be a faithful man.

Second, the fact that the qualifications for overseers follow immediately on the heels of Paul's injunctions concerning women in the church, suggests that when he prohibited women from teaching and exercising authority over men, he may have had eldership in mind. A closer look at eldership in 1 Timothy reveals that the two unique functions given to elders are teaching (3:2) and ruling (5:17)–the two activities specifically denied to women in the church. It seems that Paul's command in 2:11-12 essentially, not to mention functionally, prohibits women from serving as elders.

Observation #3: Women served in Diaconal Functions

1Timothy 3:11 is the center of no small amount of controversy. Some translations make the subject of the sentence to be "their wives" others give it as "women." The Greek word is *gynaikas,* which can mean "women" or "wives" depending on the context. If the word means "their wives," then Paul is commanding the deacons' wives to be noble women. If, however, the word is better understood as "women," then it looks as if Paul is giving the qualifications for deaconesses, or at least a subset of the office of deacon that could be filled by women.

In support of the first view it can be argued: (1) It would be strange for Paul to introduce another office right in the middle of his instructions for deacons. Verse 12 goes back to deacons again, so it makes more sense that verse 11 is another requirement for deacons. (2) If Paul were giving requirements for deaconesses you would think that he would include something about their families, about being a one man woman. (3) The reason the character of elders' wives is not mentioned is because the wives of elders would not assist in their teaching-ruling ministry in the same way that the wives of deacons would help in their service work. This explains why Paul gives instructions to deacon wives, but not to elder wives.

In support of the second view it can be argued: (1) The wording in verses 8 and 11 is the same. Verse 8 begins, literally, "deacons likewise must be dignified" (*diakonous osautos semnous*). Verse 11 begins, literally, "women likewise must be dignified" (*gynaikas osautos semnas*). Verse 11 seems to be introducing another office like verse 8 did. (2) The word *gynaikas* is literally "women." And though it can be translated "wives," Paul could have made that clear by adding a possessive pronoun (i.e *their* wives"). Greek does not have to include possessive pronouns for the idea to be present (which is why the ESV and NIV, for example, translate *gynaikas* as "their wives"), but why would Paul be so ambiguous as to leave out "their" at such a crucial spot? (3) Why would Paul include qualifications for deacon wives but not the elder wives? Is it okay for elders to have undignified, unfaithful wives?

There is no way of knowing for sure which understanding of *gynaikas* Paul has in mind (although I lean toward the second view). In the end, however, the practical application is probably not any different. Whether the verse is talking about wives who help their husbands in their diaconal work, or about women doing diaconal work as deaconesses, the outcome is the same: women are doing diaconal kinds of work. There is nothing in the nature of diaconal-service ministry to preclude, by necessity, a woman serving as a deaconess. Phoebe was a *diaconos* after all (Rom. 16:1).

My biblically informed hunch is that the early church knew two offices, elder and deacon, but that women from the beginning worked alongside deacons, performing many of the same functions and serving in similar roles. Granted, today many churches accord ruling authority to deacons (in some contexts deacons function more like elders). But in so far as diaconal ministry is service oriented, as it seems to be in the New Testament, deacon type work is completely open to women.

CHAPTER NINE

COMMON OBJECTIONS

There are many objections to the understanding of Genesis, the Gospels, 1 Corinthians 11, 1 Corinthians 14, and 1 Timothy 2 and 3 which I have just laid out. Let me respond to eight of the most common.

Objection 1: Galatians 3:28 - "There is neither Jew nor Greek, there is neither slave nor free, there is neither male nor female, for you are all one in Christ Jesus."

For egalitarians this text is the gold standard for settling the question of gender roles in the church. While Paul's teachings in 1 Corinthians and 1 Timothy were more occasional, they argue, this is clearly transcultural. Galatians 3:28 is *the* verse. Nothing can be understood about men and women apart from it and every verse must go through it in order to have validity.

But aside from the questionable approach of making this verse the final word on the subject, does this verse actually teach what egalitarians claim? Does Galatians 3:28 obliterate gender-specific roles in the church?

Entire books have been written about this one verse, but the simple answer is "No." Galatians 3:28 does not abolish gender-specific roles in the church. The equality Paul champions in 3:28 has little or nothing to do with roles in the church and everything to do with spiritual status before God.

Consider the broader context of Galatians. Paul is trying to forge a theological path through the Jew-Gentile controversy ravaging the church. The main issue at stake is whether Gentiles have to start living like Jews in order to be saved. This in turn brings Paul back to the larger question of what it means to be a true "Jew" in the first place. Do we receive the Spirit by the law or by believing (3:2)? Are we justified by the law or through faith (2:16)? Paul's clear answer is that we are declared right before God through faith in Christ.

But some Jews were in danger of missing the boat. Peter, for example, had to be rebuked because he refused table fellowship with Gentiles (Gal. 2:11-14). Apparently some in Galatia were making the similar error of thinking the Jews and Gentiles were on a different spiritual plane. Against this error, Paul strenuously argues that we are all one in

Christ. There is neither Jew nor Greek, slave nor free, male nor female.

So what does it mean that we are all one? In what way is there neither male nor female? Does gender cease to matter for those in Christ? Certainly not, or monogamous heterosexual marriage (one man joined with one woman) would be in jeopardy. Paul is not obliterating gender-specific roles. His notion of equality means something different. Men and women are equal in that both were held prisoners under the law (3:23); both are justified by faith (verse 24); both are set free from the bonds of the law (verse 25); both are sons of God in Christ (verse 26); both are clothed in Christ (verse 27); and both belong to Christ as heirs according to the promise (verse 29). Paul's point is not that gender is abolished in Christ, but that gender neither gets one closer to God nor makes one farther from him.

Objection 2: Ephesians 5:21 - "Submit to one another out of reverence for Christ." (NIV)

Some Christians try to minimize any distinctions between men and women by appealing to mutual submission. After all, doesn't God enjoin us to "submit to one another out of reverence for Christ"? Certainly he does. But what is meant by mutual submission? Surely no one will deny that we are to love one another, prefer others above ourselves, deal gently with each other, respond kindly, and treat others with respect and humility. If that's what we mean by mutual submission, I'm all for it.

But egalitarians go further, maintaining that mutual submission cancels out any structure of authority, so that men and women really submit to one another, which means that whatever authority exists in the marriage is completely reciprocal.

As attractive as this sounds, there are a number of problems with this view. First, if we are consistent with the logic of mutual submission as mutual deference throughout Ephesians 5 and 6, we will put parents in a bit of a bind. If all believers ought to submit to one another out of reverence for Christ, and therefore husbands do not really have authority over their wives, then neither would parents really have authority over their children (Eph. 6:1). If mutual submission cancels authoritative relationships for the one, it does for the other.

Moreover, the context suggests a different meaning altogether. Following the injunction to submit to one another, Paul outlines the proper relationship between different parties. Wives should submit to husbands; children obey their parents; and slaves obey their masters. Paul has in mind specific roles when he commands mutual submission. His concern is not that everyone deal graciously and respectfully with one another (though, that's a good idea too), but that Christians submit to those who are in authority over them: wives to husbands, children to parents, slaves to masters. Submitting to one another out of reverence for Christ means that we submit to those whose position entails authority over us.

Any other meaning of Ephesians 5:21 does not do justice to the Greek. The word for submission (*hypotasso*) is never in used in the New Testament as a generic love and respect for others. The word *hypotasso* occurs thirty-seven times in the New Testament outside of Ephesians 5:21, always with reference to a relationship where one party has authority over another. Thus, Jesus submits (*hypotasso*) to his parents (Luke 2:51), demons to the disciples (Luke 10:17, 20), the flesh to the law (Rom. 8:7), creation to futility (Rom. 8:20), the Jews to God's righteousness (Rom. 10:3), citizens to their rulers and governing officials (Rom. 13:1, 5; Titus 3:1; 1 Peter 2:13), spirit of the prophets to the prophets (1 Cor. 14:32), women in the churches (1 Cor. 14:34), Christians to God (Heb. 12:9; James 4:7), all things to Christ or God (1 Cor. 15:27, 28; Eph. 1:22; Phil. 3:21; Hebrews 2:5, 8; 1 Peter 3:22), the Son to God (1 Cor. 15:28), wives to husbands (Eph. 5:24; Col. 3:18; 1 Peter 3:1, 5), slaves to masters (Titus 2:9; 1 Peter 2:18); the younger to their elders (1 Peter 5:5), and Christians to gospel workers (1 Cor. 16:16). Nowhere in the New Testament does *hypotasso* refer to the reciprocal virtues of patience, kindness, and humility. It is always and only used for relationships where one party has authority over another.

Objection 3: Slavery

Egalitarians rightly notice that side by side with many of the New Testament commands for female submission are commands for slaves and masters.

They go on to argue that if one is cultural, the other must be cultural. God did not create slavery or patriarchy; he simply regulated them. Moreover, instead of explicitly overturning these patterns, the New Testament encourages equality and respect among all people, sowing the seeds for the full emancipation of women and slaves in the future.

Or so the argument goes. But is it a good one? Does the equation work: Slavery was regulated in the Bible and then later abolished; consequently, headship which was regulated in the Bible should now also be abolished?

This is a fair question and one that must be dealt with. The best way to approach this objection is to do an honest assessment of the Bible's take on slavery. If I had to summarize the Bible's treatment of slavery in a sentence, I would put it this way: The Bible does not condemn slavery, nor does it condone it.

Let's start with the first half of that sentence. Why doesn't the Bible condemn slavery in no uncertain terms? In trying to answer that question, we need to remember that slavery in the ancient world was not about race. Here in America, you can't talk about slavery without talking about blacks and whites. But that wasn't the context in the ancient world. Slavery was a lot of things, but it wasn't a race thing. Nevertheless, why didn't Paul, or Jesus for that matter, denounce the institution of slavery? Were they chicken, too cowardly to rock the boat? That doesn't fit Paul or Jesus. I don't think we can say they were simply too scared or too pragmatic to rebuke the status quo. So why don't Jesus and Paul condemn slavery outright?

Two reasons. First, because their goal was not political and social revolution. To be sure, political and social change followed in their wake, but their primary goal was spiritual. They proclaimed a message of faith and repentance and reconciliation with God. Where this message had political ramifications, so be it. But Jesus and Paul were not first of all political and social reformers. Jesus taught the way of the kingdom and proclaimed himself to be the Messiah. And Paul taught the way of the kingdom through Jesus the Christ. That was the subject of their preaching. They simply did not comment on every political and social issue of the day. More preachers, from the right and from the left in this country, would do well to follow their example.

The second reason I believe Jesus and Paul did not condemn slavery outright is because slavery in the ancient world was not always undesirable. Scholars disagree as to whether slavery in the Roman Empire was mostly harsh or mostly lenient. No doubt, it could be both. But here's how *The International Standard Bible Encyclopedia* describes slavery at the time of the New Testament:

> Large numbers of people sold themselves into slavery for various reasons, above all to enter a life that was easier and more secure than existence as a poor, freeborn person...Many non-Romans sold themselves to Roman citizens with the justified expectation, carefully regulated by

Roman law, of becoming Roman citizens themselves when manumitted...Certainly, capable
slaves had an advantage over their free counter-
parts in that they were often given an excellent
education at their owner's expense...Such slaves
did not have to wait until manumission before
they were capable of establishing friendships
with their owners and other free persons as human beings...For many, self-sale into slavery with
anticipation of manumission was regarded as the
most direct means to be integrated into Greek
and Roman society. As such, in stark contrast
to New World slavery in the 17th-19th cents.,
Greco-Roman slavery functioned as a process
rather than a permanent condition.

—EN 14

We don't want to paint too rosy a picture. Masters could treat their slaves cruelly, harshly, and in-
humanely. But it is important to realize that slavery
was a manageable way out of dire poverty for many
people. One of the big differences between slavery in
the ancient world and slavery of the 17th, 18th, and
19th centuries, was that slavery in the ancient world
was often not permanent. In the Old Testament, for
example, there were a number of ways for slaves to
gain their freedoms. In some circumstances, you
were set free after six years. Other times, a relative
could purchase your freedom or you could purchase
it yourself. And at the Year of Jubilee, Hebrew slaves
were released and received back their inheritance.
The Old Testament regulated slavery in a number of
ways, without ever explicitly condemning it.

But let me be clear: while the Bible does not condemn slavery outright, it never condones it, and it certainly never commends it. Slavery is not a creation ordinance like marriage (EN 15). Slavery is not celebrated as a God-given gift like children are. Slavery was not pronounced good before the Fall like work was.

Slavery is never rooted in God's good purposes for his creation. In fact, slavery as it developed in many parts of the New World would have been outlawed in the Old Testament. "Whoever steals a man and sells him, and anyone found in possession of him, shall be put to death" (Ex. 21:16). That command alone would not allow for anything like the African slave-trade. Likewise, 1 Timothy 1:8-10: "Now we know that the law is good, if one uses it lawfully, understanding this, that the law is not laid down for the just but for the lawless and disobedient, for the ungodly and sinners, for the unholy and profane, for those who strike their fathers and mothers, for murderers, the sexually immoral, men who practice homosexuality, *enslavers*, liars, perjurers, and whatever else is contrary to sound doctrine (emphasis added)." The Bible clearly condemns taking someone captive and selling him into slavery.

And while Paul did not encourage widespread political revolution and the overthrow of the institution of slavery, he did encourage slaves to gain their freedom if possible. "Each one should remain in the condition in which he was called. Were you a slave when called? Do not be concerned about it. But if you can gain your freedom, avail yourself of the opportunity" (1 Cor. 7:20-21). When Paul sent the runaway slave turned Christian, Onesimus, back to his Christian master, Philemon, Paul gave Philemon this advice, "For this perhaps is why he was parted from you for a while, that you might have him back forever, no longer as a slave but more than a slave, as a beloved brother—especially to me, but how much more to you, both in the flesh and in the Lord" (Philem. 15-16). So, far from commending slavery as an inherent good, Paul encouraged slaves to gain their freedom if possible. Additionally, he exhorted masters, if Philemon is any example, to welcome their slaves, not as slaves, but as brothers.

The bottom line is that the Bible, without commending it to us, regulates the institution of slavery where it exists. Imagine if Paul were writing to families today. He would, no doubt, address husbands and wives, children and parents, and then he might address children and their step-dads. "Children obey your step-dads, for this is right in the Lord. Step-dads, love your step-children as if they were your very own. For God loves you though you once did not belong to him." If that's what Paul wrote to us, we would know how children and step-dads should relate to each other. But we wouldn't have any warrant for thinking that Paul commends divorce and remarriage. And we wouldn't have any warrant for thinking that Paul condemns every step-dad everywhere. We would realize he is not commenting one way or the other on the situation. He is simply regulating it where it exists, because divorce and remarriage, like slavery, is not God's design for the family. There is much in the Bible that would speak against it, but it is not, in every circumstance, an inherent evil. So I imagine Paul would regulate the relationship between step-children and step-parents just like he regulated the practice of slavery: give instructions to make it more liveable without explicitly condemning or condoning it.

Objection 4: Women in Ministry

"What about all the women engaged in ministry in the Bible?" some may ask. Women in ministry is not the problem. The problem is women in inappropriate positions of ministry. Egalitarians, of course, argue that there are no inappropriate roles for women. To bolster their claim, they point to what they see as a myriad of women throughout the Bible in leadership roles. 1 Timothy 2, they say, must be directed specifically for the situation in Ephesus because a number of women throughout the Bible taught and exercised authority over men.

Let's look briefly at several of the most common examples and see if these woman exercised the kind of authority and engaged in the kind of teaching prohibited by Paul.

Deborah. Deborah seems to be a glaring exception to the rule laid out in 1 Timothy 2. She was a prophetess, a judge, and oversaw a period of victory and peace in Israel (Judg. 4-5). But several considerations mitigate against making too much of

Deborah's judgeship. First, she seems to be the only judge with no military function. Deborah, instead, is instructed to send for Barak (a man) to conduct the military maneuvers (4:5-7). Even when Deborah goes with Barak into battle, he is the one who leads the 10,000 men into the fray (4:10, 14ff.). Second, Barak is rebuked for insisting that Deborah go with him in the first place. Deborah willingly handed over the leadership to Barak and then shamed him for his hesitation (4:9). Hence, the glory would not go to Barak but to Jael, the wife of Heber the Kenite (4:9, 22). Third, whatever sort of authority Deborah shared with Barak, it was not a priestly, or teaching authority.

Prophetesses. Besides Deborah, several other women are called prophetesses in the Old and New Testaments: Miriam (Ex. 15:20), Huldah (2 Kings 22:14), Noadiah (Neh. 6:14), Anna (Luke 2:36), Philip's daughters (Acts 21:8-9). Two comments may help put the ministry of prophetesses in its proper context. First, recall that New Testament prophecy did not carry the same authority as Old Testament prophecy. Congregational prophets in the New Testament were given occasional Spirit-prompted utterances that needed to be weighed against accepted teaching. Which is to say that Philip's daughters and the prophets at Corinth were not the same as preachers or authoritative teachers. Second, in the Old Testament, where prophecy carries absolute authority, we see women prophetesses carrying out their ministry differently than male prophets.

Miriam ministered to women (Ex. 15:20), and Deborah and Huldah prophesied more privately than publicly. In contrast to prophets like Isaiah or Jeremiah who publicly declared the word of the Lord for all to hear, Deborah judged among those who came to her in private (Judg. 4:5) and instructed Barak individually, while Huldah prophesied privately to the messengers Josiah sent to her (2 Kings 22:14-20). Noadiah, the only other prophetess mentioned in the Old Testament, opposed Nehemiah along with the wicked prophet Shemaiah. The example of Noadiah, disobedient as she was, tells us nothing about God's design for women in ministry.

Priscilla. Mentioned three times in the book of Acts and three times in the Epistles, Priscilla/Prisca was obviously well known in the early church (Acts 18:2, 18, 26; Rom. 16:3; 1 Cor. 16:19; 2 Tim. 4:19). She is most often listed first before her husband Aquilla, which may or may not be significant. Perhaps because she was the more prominent of the two, or maybe she converted before her husband, or maybe the disciples just got to know her first (like when you are friends with Sally for a long time and then she marries Joe so you refer to them as "Sally and Joe"). In any case, together, they instructed the influential teacher Apollos. But again, this teaching was done in private (Acts 18:26). Priscilla may have been learned, wise, and influential, but there is no indication that she exercised teaching-authority over men.

Phoebe. Paul commends Phoebe to the Romans as a *diakonos* of the church in Cenchrea (Rom. 16:1). This may mean that Phoebe was a deaconess or that she was more generally a servant. The word itself is ambiguous. In either case, there is no indication that Phoebe the servant was a teacher or leader over men.

Junia. Paul gives Andronicus and Junia greetings, hailing them as "outstanding among the apostles" (Rom. 16:7). Egalitarians often use this verse to argue that a women can exercise authority over men because Junia (a woman) was an apostle. This is a thin argument for several reasons. First, it is possible that Junia (*iounian* in Greek) is a man, not a woman. Second, "outstanding among the apostles" suggests that Junia was held in esteem by the apostles, not that she was an apostle. Third, even if Junia was a woman and was an apostle, it is not clear that she was an apostle like the Twelve. "Apostle" can be used in a less technical sense as a messenger or representative (2 Cor. 8:23; Phil. 2:25).

Euodia and *Syntyche*. Euodia and Syntyche (both women) were fellow workers with Paul, who contended at his side in the cause of the gospel (Phil. 4:3). Nothing here implies teaching or authority over men. There are hundreds of way to work for the cause of this gospel without leading or teaching. Without apology, we ought to fully affirm the important work Euodia and Syntyche performed, and millions of women continue to do, in the cause of the gospel, without thinking that their presence in ministry somehow overturns the biblical teaching on men and women in the church.

Chosen Lady. Some maintain that the "chosen lady" in 2 John is the pastor/elder of the church. The chosen lady, however, is not the pastor of the church; she is the church. Not only is the letter much too general to be addressed to a specific person (cf. 3 John), and not only is female imagery often used of the church (cf. Eph. 5; Rev 12), but, most decisively, John uses the second person plural throughout 2 John, indicating that he does not have an individual in mind, but a body of believers (verses 6, 8, 10, 12).

Objection 5: The Priesthood of All Believers

It is sometimes argued that the priesthood of all believers nullifies any authority structures in the church, certainly male-only authority structures. Two points can be made against this objection.

First, Christians, of all people, should not be anti-authority. The Bible doesn't use authority as a dirty word. Many Christians, some for rebellious reasons and some for understandable reasons, feel that authority is, if not inherently, at least inevitably, oppressive. Granted, authority on a number of different levels is often abused and Bible passages granting authority are often abused too. I take that seriously. But nearly every passage of Scripture has been abused at one time or another. That's why we have legalists and antinomians. It's hard work to keep complex truths in balance.

While the Bible has plenty of examples of authority gone amuck (the Bible has examples of every good gift gone amuck), it never denigrates authority per se. We see authority structures honored in society (Rom. 13:1-7), in the family (husbands/wives, children/parents), and in the church (Heb. 13:17). We see an authority relationship between the Father and the Son in the incarnation, if not from all eternity. And most obviously, we live our lives under God's authority, which is absolute without ever being tyrannical or oppressive. Authority structures are not the problem; sinful people in those structures are.

Second, while the priesthood of all believers means that all Christians have gifts and ministries, it does not mean that there are no leaders in the church, nor does it mean that these leaders shouldn't be only men. I've heard it said that "Yes, yes, the priests in the Old Testament were all male, but that has no bearing on New Testament leadership models, because now we are all 'a royal priesthood' and 'holy nation'" (1 Peter 2:9). It is true that we–women as well as men–are a royal priesthood. But Peter's New Testament description of the church was simply a reiteration of God's word given to the people at Sinai when he declared "you shall be to me a kingdom of priests and a holy nation" (Ex. 19:6). The priesthood of all believers is an Old Testament idea. And if an all-male priesthood was consistent with an every person kingdom of priests in the Old Testament, there is no reason to think that an all-male eldership is inconsistent with the priesthood of believers in the New Testament.

Objection 6: Representation

Another argument sometimes offered in support of women in church office is that it would provide for better representation among the leadership. The best leadership team, it is said, will be a sampling from different groups in the church–some old, some young, some faithful members, some on the fringe, some male and some female. After all, how are we to know how to minister to women (or any other group) if we don't know what they think?

Listening to the people in our churches is certainly a good idea. And there's a lot of wisdom in being aware of the make-up of those in leadership. We all have blindspots. Men overlook some things that women don't. Parents with small children will be attuned to certain needs that empty-nesters might miss. It makes good sense to be aware of the perspectives beyond the few who are in formal leadership. It is true that most elders and pastors can do a better job of soliciting input from various circles. They can host church-wide town hall meetings, or open forums, or bring in "consultants" from within the congregation to help cast the vision or make an important decision. It is certainly wise to "make plans by seeking advice" (Prov. 20:18 NIV). For "without counsel plans fail, but with many advisers they succeed" (Prov. 15:22).

But the church is not a democracy. The elders or pastors are not representative of church interest groups as much as they are representative of Christ. Church officers are not like senators representing various constituencies. They are given the keys of the kingdom to lead the church as Christ would. The idea that church governing structures should mirror the make-up of the congregation owes more to American sensibilities than biblical reflection. Israel had a male-only priesthood. Jesus had a male-only apostolic band. Paul appointed faithful men to teach others (2 Tim. 2:2). By no means do I wish to alienate women, but the business of church leadership is not *primarily* listening to what the congregation has to say; it is hearing what God has said and passing it on.

I desire a teachable spirit and humble heart. I will be the first to admit that I don't have all the answers, nor does every good idea come from my brain. I want to listen. Yet, I can't help but think that the church has swallowed too much of our culture's perspectivalism. We have categorized and sub-categorized the human race into every conceivable box until we are so fragmented that we wonder whether anyone can understand anything about anyone else. And consequently, we have come to believe that no one can be fully valued or genuinely helped without their perspective at the table.

No doubt, a woman would add a different perspective. So would a teenager, or a seeker, or a new convert, or a disgruntled member, but perspective is not the main issue. If we need to know each person in each unique situation before ministering effectively, we will be left with very small churches. You do not need to be a recovering alcoholic to minister to one, nor do you have to have been a rebellious teenager in order to be helpful to youth.

To be sure, life experience does matter, which is why the elders and pastors are not the only ones doing ministry in the church. Women (to name just one "category") should be ministering in all sorts of situations. There are some important areas of ministry where women are uniquely qualified and should, frankly, take over the work from men, because they will do it better. But leadership over men is not one of them, not because women would do miserably, but because God has not designed it that way.

One final note. It is no small thing that the men in leadership, if they are married, will have already proven that they know how to lead and care for their wives (1 Tim. 3:4-5). If men have not demonstrated a loving sensitive leadership in their families, they should not lead anyone, male or female. Hopefully, an elder board filled with godly men will have the maturity, wisdom, and sensitivity to lead a church in a way that honors, cherishes, and encourages women—even if women do not have their "perspective" at the table.

Objection 7: We Don't Have Any Good Men!

This is a real problem in some churches. Good men are nowhere to be found. But I would argue that, in some cases, the lack of good, willing men is the result of years of encouraging women into positions of leadership that should be filled by men. Sadly, if given the chance, most men will gladly abdicate their responsibility to be mature leaders in the church and in the home.

In other instances, a church may be so small or so new that men who meet the standards of 1 Timothy 3 are nowhere to be found. I remember Elisabeth Elliot facing this problem when she served as a missionary in South America for a time after her husband Jim was martyred. She advocated women sharing the gospel one on one with men until these men were able to lead the rest. In other words, if there are absolutely no qualified men anywhere, like in frontier missions where there are no Christians period, women should share the gospel and even do some personal teaching (as Priscilla with Apollos), but they should not assume authoritative leadership over the people. There is a way for the men to be built up for leadership, even by women, without the women taking unbiblical positions of authority.

Objection 8: Gifts and Calling

Women have vital spiritual gifts. No one is denying that. Women can even have gifts of teaching and leadership. We all know women who are great organizers, administrators, communicators, and leaders. No one wants to waste those gifts. But the Bible stipulates certain ways in which these gifts are to be used. Women can, and should, exercise powerful gifts of teaching, provided it is not over men. Surely, teaching children and other women is not a waste of a woman's gifts?

Moreover, the fact that people have benefitted from women's gifts wrongly used (having teaching authority over men) is an argument based on effect more than obedience. That God uses us at all, when we as a church seem to stray from his word so frequently, is a testimony to God's grace, not a blueprint for ministry. God has blessed the public teaching of women over men despite themselves, just as God has used me to bless others despite myself. The goal in both cases, hopefully, is to know the truth more clearly and approximate it more nearly. "But it works" is the wrong measure of our faithfulness.

Similarly, the appeal to calling is not very convincing. In April 2003, *First Things,* a conservative Roman Catholic periodical, ran an essay called "Ordaining Women: Two Views." Sarah Hinlicky Wilson concluded her piece in favor of women's ordination by appealing to a sense of calling.

> Much has been said here of why there is no reason *not* to ordain women. A word or two as to why it *should* be done is yet needed...As Sister Thekla once said, "The only justification for the monastic life lies simply in the fact that God calls some people to it." By the same token, the only justification for the ordination of women lies in the fact that God calls some women to it.
>
> —EN 16

To be sure, many women, like this author, have felt a sense of call to ordained ministry. But God's objective revelation in Scripture must have priority over our subjective understanding of God's will for our lives. Though a call may be honestly felt, such an appeal is hopelessly subjective. In fact, men and women in ministry would do well to stop couching their ministerial authority in some experiential call. Not only does it run the risk of creating an unhealthy sacred-secular dichotomy ("have you been 'called' or are you just a plumber?"), but more important than a sense of call is whether or not your ministry has proved fruitful in the past, the church recognizes and affirms your gifts, and you meet the scriptural requirements. I have no problem with people referring to their vocation, pastoral or otherwise, as a "calling," if by the term they simply mean to acknowledge a spiritual purpose in their work. But as a decision-making tool, finding one's "calling" is an unsure guide.

At the very least, even if the "calling" terminology is appropriate, it must never be allowed to trump the objective standards of Scripture. If a sense of internal call to preach is the undeniable sign of the Spirit's leading, we should applaud those who have laid hands of ordination on gay priests, pastors, and bishops. If a sense of calling and giftedness is the most basic prerequisite for ministry, who are we to refuse the homosexual sensing a call the opportunity to fulfill his or her God-given potential? And what about the young man who feels a call to pastoral ministry but is not very good with people and can't articulate his faith to others? Should we allow his "call" to override scriptural qualifications? A better approach is to gently and firmly redirect Christian men and women in our flock who have somewhat innocently, but also wrongly, "sensed" their way into pastures that our Good Shepherd did not intend for them (EN 17).

CHAPTER TEN

LIFE TOGETHER
IN THE CHURCH

So what? Where does all of this exegesis and theology leave us? How does this work out in the
church?

I'll get to the application soon enough, but we
must understand the principle first. Far too often,
egalitarians demean the complementarian position
by jumping to all sorts of undesirable applications.
"Well, then women can't teach any Sunday School."
"Women shouldn't sing in the choir I suppose." "I
guess that means women shouldn't be missionaries."
That sort of approach, besides being unfair, puts
the cart before the horse. We shouldn't invalidate
principle by application when we don't know yet
what the principle is!

When considering the freedom and boundaries
for women in the church, my principle is simply

this: *I encourage women to serve the Lord in any and all avenues of ministry except those which involve teaching and authority over men.*

So what about real life where men and women and churches struggle in getting to this principle and then struggle some more in applying it? How does one walk the walk from all this exegetical talk?

Freedom and Boundaries in Process

As I stated earlier, I believe it is unwise and impractical for churches to limp between two opinions on this subject. This issue is not the type that can be left alone. We must come to biblically informed conclusions. But communicating these convictions will require a different approach in different churches. There is no one-size fits all model when it comes to sorting through the strange mix of biblical texts, people's feelings, and theological fidelity. Oftentimes, I can't even figure out what's best in my own church, let alone someone else's. But I can share what my intended pastoral process looks like.

1. The church leadership needs to study this issue. The elders, or whomever is charged with overseeing the doctrine and teaching of the church, should biblically and prayerfully investigate this issue. I've written this book in hopes that it would be of help to churches and leaders going through such a process.
2. If the leadership affirms the existence of role distinctions for men and women in

the church, the next step is to present their complementarian convictions to the congregation. The members of the church should have ample opportunity, in different venues (one on one, question and answer times, etc.), to respond and ask questions. Be as transparent as possible. This issue is controversial enough without people feeling as though the leadership did an end-around or pulled this decision out of thin air. Lead, but listen as you lead.

3. Unless the issue is really "open," do not pretend it is. It is manipulative and dishonest for the leadership to present the issue before the congregation for fact-finding, discovery, and group discernment, when the leaders have already decided what they believe and where they want the church to go. Besides, to ask dozens or hundreds of people to come to a shared consensus on their own with an issue like this is, in my opinion, poor leadership, not to mention nearly impossible.

4. The pastors and elders, or whomever constitutes the recognized leadership, should gently, but firmly try to persuade the congregation as to what the Bible teaches about gender roles in the church. If the issue has never been officially defined before, some people may leave the church. That is not the end of the world, but neither is it our goal. However inefficient and painful it may be,

special care should be given to those who disagree.

5. The church, or its leaders (depending on one's polity), should adopt a statement clarifying its stance on women in the church. The Affirmation section of The Danvers Statement (Appendix 3) is a good option for those who aren't eager to reinvent the wheel.

6. My suggestion is that there be two different sets of boundaries when it comes to affirming a complementarian view of gender roles. I do not believe complementarianism should make its way into statements of faith which define church membership. Egalitarians are my brothers and sisters in the Lord and I could not in good conscience exclude them from church membership. Leadership, however, is a different matter. I think it best to include a complementarian view of gender in some statement of official church doctrine. Depending on the situation, the leadership could be asked to affirm the church's position, or at the very least, recognize the position of the church and be asked to refrain from advocating otherwise (EN 18). This may be a tough pill to swallow for those who were used to more ambivalence, but in the long run it wili be more divisive to leave this issue undefined and be forced to revisit it every two years. It would be much better for new members, new leaders, and new staff

to know where the church stands and what is expected of them.

7. Pray before, during, and after the process for humility, wisdom, courage and grace.

Freedom and Boundaries in Practice

Function matters more than title. What we call women in their roles is not the main issue. I am more concerned with whether women are filling roles which exercise teaching authority over men. This means ordination is not the main thing. Men and women can be ordained to all sorts of worthy tasks so long as these tasks are consistent with the roles outlined in Scripture. Practically, this means that women should not be elders or preaching pastors. Now, it may very well be that some of the things elders typically do in our churches are not specifically or uniquely elder duties, and consequently, women may be able to do some "elder-ly" things, like call on shut-ins, greet people at the door, pray with people after the service, visit single moms, or counsel a pregnant teenager. But to be an elder/pastor, by definition, is to be a teacher and in a position of spiritual authority. These roles are not open to women.

I believe women can still teach–children and women–just not men. Many will ask at what age, then, do boys become men. That's not an easy question and will change somewhat from culture to culture. But it seems to me that as long as a male is still under the authority of his parents (up through high school for sure), it is not inappropriate for him to be under the teaching authority of a woman. Once he is no longer under parental authority (perhaps in college or living on his own), he should be instructed in the Scriptures by men.

I realize there are all sorts of fine lines to be worked out. For example, I would not support a woman teaching a mixed adult Sunday school class on Romans. I would be okay, however, with a woman leading a time of prayer in mixed company. I would gladly support a woman facilitating a small group Bible study or leading a book discussion or chairing a committee. Praying in church or giving the announcements or sharing a testimony or singing a solo is certainly appropriate. On the other hand, preaching or teaching in corporate worship clearly is not. Some of these are judgment calls, I know. Other complementarians may disagree. I am simply trying to best discern what constitutes authority and teaching and what does not.

Finally, we need to do a better job encouraging women to do ministry. This cannot be an afterthought, a nice sounding sentiment meant to get those who disagree with us off our backs. The position of elder may not be open to women, but there are thousands of other areas that are. Women can minister to the sick, the dying, the mentally impaired, and the physically handicapped. They can share their faith, share their resources, and open their home to strangers. They can write, counsel, mentor, organize, administrate, design, plan, and come alongside others. They can pray. They can minister to single moms, new moms, breast cancers survivors, and abuse victims. They can bring meals, sew curtains, send care packages, and throw baby showers. They can do sports ministries, lead women's Bible studies, teach systematic theology to other women, and plan missions trips. They can raise their kids to the glory of God and they can embrace singleness as a gift from God. I pray for women who love to cook and quilt and work in the nursery. I pray for women to counsel almost-divorced wives, and mentor young ladies, and teach doctrine to other women. There are a thousand things women can be doing in ministry beside the few roles the Bible does not permit them to fill. We need to make this point abundantly and repetitively clear.

The Fruit of Freedom within the Beauty of Boundaries

More work will need to be done in each particular context in terms of applying a complementarian vision of manhood and womanhood to the church. I have just scratched the surface of what it might look like. Please, though, do not be quick to reject complementarianism just because the application seems difficult or controversial. Our first and most important question is always: "What has God said?" God's word is precious wisdom, a choice jewel, and sweet honey to our lips. His will is always right, always trustworthy, and always good.

Dr. Dorothy Patterson, a strong complementarian who has been active in ministry for years, admits that for many women, 1 Timothy 2 is a "hard word." But, she also finds "in Scripture a 'sure word' that frees me to offer to the Father whatever giftedness or creativity I may have as well as my personal energies and passions—whether in teaching biblical truth, extending Christian hospitality, or engaging in individual ministries." But these energies and passions must always take shape within the clear mandates of Scripture. "As a believing woman I do not feel a freedom to allow my theological training or giftedness for ministry to elevate personal experience, modern cultural perception, or ministry opportunities above biblical boundaries" (EN 19). She finds freedom in obedience and protection in serving the Lord on his terms.

Like Patterson and scores of other men and women, I am not a complementarian begrudgingly, as if I need to make excuses for God's ways. I believe in role distinctions for men and women not simply because it is right, but because I believe it is best. Happily, God made men and women to relate to each other in different ways, as one small part of what Elisabeth Elliot calls a "glorious hierarchical order of graduated splendor...a mighty universal dance, choreographed for the perfection and fulfillment of each participant" (EN 20). God's design gives us blessed boundaries along a blessed path—to follow this path is freedom, to reject it will ultimately yield frustration. In the end, a complementarian view of gender roles should be embraced not only because it is biblical, but because it brings glory to God, blessing to the church, and the full, divinely ordained meaning and purpose to manhood and womanhood.

A Sermon on
Ephesians 5:22-33
(EN 21)

[22]Wives, submit to your own husbands, as to the Lord. [23]For the husband is the head of the wife even as Christ is the head of the church, his body, and is himself its Savior. [24]Now as the church submits to Christ, so also wives should submit in everything to their husbands.

[25]Husbands, love your wives, as Christ loved the church and gave himself up for her, [26]that he might sanctify her, having cleansed her by the washing of water with the word, [27]so that he might present the church to himself in splendor, without spot or wrinkle or any such thing, that she might be holy and without blemish. [28]In the same way husbands should love their wives as their own bodies. He who loves his wife loves himself. [29]For no one ever hated his own flesh, but nourishes and cherishes it, just as Christ does the church, [30]because we are members of

his body. [31]"Therefore a man shall leave his father and mother and hold fast to his wife, and the two shall become one flesh." [32]This mystery is profound, and I am saying that it refers to Christ and the church. [33]However, let each one of you love his wife as himself, and let the wife see that she respects her husband.

In July 2004, I found a news item with the lead line: "Women Senators Balk at Controversial Nominee" (EN 22). President George W. Bush had nominated J. Leon Holmes to serve on the federal district court in Arkansas. Holmes became a controversial nominee when it was discovered that in 1997 he co-authored an article with his wife in the *Arkansas Catholic Review* in which they wrote, "the wife is to subordinate herself to the husband...the woman is to place herself under the authority of the man." Holmes claimed that the words were taken out of context. Senator Dianne Feinstein, for one, still found Holmes unacceptable: "How can I or any other American believe that one who truly believes a woman is subordinate to her spouse [can] interpret the Constitution fairly?" Republican Senators Susan Collins, Lisa Murkowski and Kay Bailey Hutchinson also objected, saying Holmes does not have a "fundamental commitment to the equality of women in our society." Holmes' nomination was eventually confirmed by the Senate 51-46.

It sounds archaic to many, if not downright sinister and un-American, but I believe that God's design for the home is a thoughtful, intelligent, gentle, submissive wife and a loving, godly, self-sacrificing, leading husband. Whether we live in the first century or the twenty-first century, Ephesians 5:22-33 is God's plan for marriage: wives submit to your husbands and husbands love your wives.

No doubt there are many objections to taking these verses at face value. What about equality? What about slavery? What about abuse? What about mutual submission? Believe it or not, there are good answers to each of these objections. On equality: the inner-workings of the Trinity show how submission does not imply inferiority or inequality. On slavery: Paul orders the relationship between slaves and masters where it exists, but never grounds the institution of slavery in God's eternal purposes. On abuse: sadly, it has happened that husbands have used these verses to justify harsh behavior toward their wives, but recent studies argue that, on the whole, patriarchal husbands are less likely to engage in domestic abuse than other kinds of husbands (EN 23). And on mutual submission: elsewhere in his letters Paul commands Christians to show mutual deference, respect, and honor, but that's not what he's advocating in Ephesians 5:21. In the New Testament, the word for "submit" (*hypotasso*) is only used for relationships where one party has authority over another.

Besides, there are many positive reasons for thinking that Ephesians 5 means what it seems to mean. For starters, there's the witness of the church. For nearly 2000 years, the church, almost without exception, has considered these verses normative for marriage. Then there's the transcultural nature of the commands. There is no indication that the commands for Ephesians 5:22-33 were culturally limited. And we could talk about the creation order. Role distinctions in marriage were not the invention of the Apostle Paul, but go back to the ordering of creation itself. And finally, there's the analogy of Christ and the church. If there is no distinction in roles, we are left with a relationship between Christ and Christ, or church and church.

But if we spend any more time proving why the text means what it seems to mean, we won't get around to actually seeing and applying what the text means.

Submission and Love: Reversing the Curse

The first thing to notice from the text itself is how the overarching commands for husbands and wives are given at their specific point of fallenness. The overarching command for wives is "submit" because that is what they find most difficult to do as sinful wives. The overarching command for husbands is "love" because that is what they find most difficult to do as sinful husbands.

The commands to submit and love are intended to reverse the curse inflicted in the Garden of Eden. God's plan from the beginning was for a gentle helping wife and a gracious leading husband. But sin corrupted God's good design. The marriage relationship was cursed: "I will surely multiply your pain in childbearing; in pain you shall bring forth children. Your desire shall be for your husband, and he shall rule over you" (Gen. 3:16).

Notice the curse on both sides of the marriage relationship in verse 16. The woman who was supposed to help and support the husband–now her desire will be for her husband. Don't misunderstand the word "desire." It does not refer to romantic desire (some curse that would be!) or a desire to please her husband; it is a desire for control. The Hebrew word for desire in 3:16 is the same word used in 4:7b "...sin is crouching at the door. Its desire is for you, but you must rule over it." The two verses have very similar verbal constructions. Genesis 4:7 (whose meaning is relatively clear) helps us understand Genesis 3:16 (whose meaning at first seems relatively unclear). Just as sin desired to have control over Cain, so the woman, tainted by sin, desires to have control over her husband. Which is why Paul gives the command "submit." The inclination of fallen woman is to rebel against her husband's authority and try to control him. Paul's command aims to reverse the effects of the curse and have Christian wives submit rather than usurp.

Likewise, men, who are supposed to lead and protect and provide for their wives, now, tainted by sin, rule over their wives. The word "rule" in 3:16 has a negative connotation. It's part of the curse. The wife becomes a usurper and the husband becomes a dictator. Again, the verbal parallels with 4:7 are telling. Sin desired to control Cain, just like the fallen wife desires to control her husband. And Cain was supposed to have mastery over sin, just like the fallen husband tries to have mastery over his wife. Under the curse, men take God's good gift of headship and twist it into tyranny. Which is why Paul gives the command "love." The inclination of fallen man is to exercise ungodly rule over his wife. Paul's command aims to reverse the effects of the curse and have Christian husbands love rather than domineer.

The Submissive Wife

But how do submission and love work out in real life? Let's start with the women. **Wives, in submitting to your husbands, support, respect, and follow them as to the Lord.**

Notice that last phrase "as to the Lord." The motivation for obedience to this command is Christ. Slaves are to obey their earthly masters as they would obey Christ (6:5). Children are to obey their parents in the Lord (6:1). And wives are to submit to their husbands as to the Lord (5:22). Submission is part of what it means to be a godly Christian wife, filled with the Spirit.

We must be careful, though. "As to the Lord" does not mean wives should submit to their husbands in exactly the same way they obey Christ. Paul never calls wives "bond-servants" of their husbands like he calls himself a "bond-servant" of Christ (Rom. 1:1 NASB). Christ is the supreme absolute authority; all other authority is only derivative. So

when Paul says wives should submit to their husbands in everything (5:24), we must let Scripture
interpret Scripture. The "in everything" does not
overturn all the other commands in Ephesians.
Wives should not steal, brawl, slander, and indulge
in every kind of impurity just because their husbands say so. The husband's authority does not
trump the authority of Christ. In submitting to
husbands, obeying parents, obeying masters, and
obeying governing authorities, we do not obey to
the point of disobeying God. As Peter says in Acts
5:29 before the Jewish leaders "We must obey God,
rather than men."

But we should not make Paul say the opposite
of what he actually says. He **does** command submission, not on the basis of shifting cultural sand, not
even on the basis of the husband's love. He roots the
command in two unchanging theological principles.
Number one, the husband is the head of the wife.
And number two, "as the church submits to Christ,
so also wives should submit in everything to their
husbands." Because of these two realities–the headship of the husband in the created order and the
analogy of Christ and the church, the wife should
freely submit to her husband.

And guys, don't miss the word "freely." The
command is for the wife, not the husband. The
man is never told to submit the wife unto himself.
Instead, the woman is told to submit herself unto
her husband. It is a submission freely given, never
forcibly taken.

Submission in Real Life

What does this submission look like? I used three verbs to describe freely given submission: wives, in submitting to your husbands, *support, respect,* and *follow* them as to the Lord.

Wives, support your husbands. God made you to be a helper for your husband (Gen. 2:18). So do all you can to encourage him as a husband, father, and worker. Come alongside him, not to control him, nor to be recognized for your service (but your husband should recognize it), but to help him. I think it is fitting, in most situations, that the wife let her husband's vocation take priority over her own. I know that is not a popular thing to say. But I think it is a fair application of what it means to be a helpmate. When a couple cannot figure how to make both of their careers a go, I think the wife should be willing to say, "I want to be a help and support to you."

Wives, respect your husbands. Most guys are all bluff. We put up a big front, but we are scared little boys inside. A husband needs to know his wife respects him as a worker, a father, and a husband. A man may get built up or torn down at work, but the words that can really make him or break him are the ones from his wife.

Give your husbands unconditional respect just as your husband ought to show you unconditional love. "Let each one of you love his wife as himself, and let the wife see that she respects her husband" (Eph. 5:33). The husband should love his wife regardless of how lovely she is, because she is as the church to him. And the wife ought to respect her husband regardless of how worthy of respect he is, because he is as Christ to her. It dishonors Christ to bad-mouth your husband, put him down to your friends, or worse yet, to your kids. Consider the way holy women of the past put their hope in God to make themselves beautiful. They were submissive to their husbands, like Sarah, who obeyed Abraham and called him her lord (1 Peter 3:5-6). Now, you don't have to call your husband "lord," but if you want to be truly beautiful, your attitude toward your husband will be like Sarah's to Abraham.

And wives, follow your husbands. Respond to his initiative. Don't second-guess him all the time. You can certainly have an opinion and should not be afraid to voice it, but don't try to undermine his authority. Provided he's not leading you into sin, follow him.

I'm thinking especially of following your husband as a spiritual leader. I could use my wife for all sorts of positive examples in this sermon, but especially in this area, I feel so fortunate. I cannot remember my wife ever refusing me, or even being put off, when I suggest we pray, or sing a hymn, or read a book together, or work our way through the Bible, or go to church. What a blessing to have a wife who gladly follows my stumbling attempts at spiritual leadership.

Trisha and I have our little squabbles like every other couple. But I can honestly say that I have never felt disrespected by my wife. And as we talk through our decisions as a couple, I have always known that if we reach an absolute impasse she will follow my leading. I feel immeasurably blessed to have a wife who is willing to follow, in what I think, is the most gracious, intelligent, strong, but gentle way possible. Twice I have moved our family from places we loved, surrounded by friends and familiarity to places that were strange and unknown, especially to my wife. And both times–when we moved from Massachusetts to Iowa and from Iowa to Michigan–my wife was terribly sad to leave. And both times we talked and prayed a lot together. And both times when it came down to making a decision my wife in effect told me "Kevin, you know I like it here, but you know that I will be okay with whatever you decide." What pain it would have brought us both if my wife's attitude had been "I'm not going to the middle of nowhere. I'm not moving away from my friends. I don't want to be around that much snow." But instead, she honored and respected and followed me better than I deserve.

The Loving Husband

And what about the men? What does Paul have to say to us? **Husbands, in loving your wives, lead, sacrifice, and care for them as Christ does for the church.**

Let's start with the last phrase again–"as Christ does for the church." The motivation for obedience to the command to love is Christ. The wife is to submit to her husband because he is, in certain ways, as Christ to her. And the husband is to love his wife for the same reason, because he is, in certain ways, as Christ to her. Men, your number one command in marriage is to love like Jesus.

The verb "love," like the verb "submit" is given not taken. The wife does not manipulate or demand love from her husband. The husband freely and unconditionally shows love to his wife. In both commands–submit and love–the focus is on what we give, not on what we get. The problem with so many books on marriage is that they focus on what we need to get out of marriage instead of telling us what we need to give in marriage. I have read numerous Christian books on marriage which do nothing but appeal to self-interest. They give us great insight on how to be loved, how our needs can be met, how our love tanks can be filled. The basic philosophy is "I'll scratch your back, because then you'll scratch mine." The mindset is love in order to be loved. But, as Jesus says, "if you love those who love you, what reward do you have? Do not even the tax collectors do the same?" (Matthew 5:46). I dare say that the Christian approach to marriage is not "his needs, her needs," but "his opportunity to honor Christ, her opportunity to honor Christ." The wife submits as to the Lord, and the husband loves as Christ to the Church.

Love in Real Life

So, once again, what does this look like? I gave three descriptive verbs: husbands, in loving your

141

wives, *lead, sacrifice,* and *provide* for them as Christ does for the church.

Husbands, lead your wives. I believe this should be true in general. The husband should be the one who most often says, "let's." "Honey, let's go on a walk." "Let's order out." "Let's pray together." "Let's get the kids ready for bed." Take the initiative, men. Do something. Don't just talk about a date-night. Plan the whole thing. Get a babysitter. Your wife may be a better organizer, a better speaker, a brighter mind, but you can still be a leader. The husband ought to be the one primarily taking the initiative, not as a tyrant, but as the head of his wife.

But that's not mainly what Ephesians 5 is about–dates and walks and such. The leadership most in view, husbands, is spiritual leadership. Christian husbands often have one of two problems: either they are dictators bossing their wives around, or they are doormats–overly passive, neutered, so-called men. They feel macho because they make a lot of money, play tackle football, or shoot things, but when it comes to loving leadership in the home, they're doormats. They take zero responsibility for the spiritual well-being of their household.

And yet, God holds us accountable for the spiritual welfare of our wives. "Love your wives, as Christ loved the church and gave himself up for her, that he might sanctify her, having cleansed her by the washing with water with the word, so that he might present the church to himself in splendor, without spot or wrinkle or any such thing, that she might be holy and without blemish." Did you catch all that? You, men, have a responsibility for your wife's holiness. Her marriage to you should be an instrument of edification, purification, and sanctification. Not sanctifying because you're so hard to live with (along the lines of "whatever doesn't kill you makes you stronger"); sanctifying because you are a spiritual leader, praying, reading, singing with your wife.

And being a spiritual leader, husbands, means you take the initiative to repair the breach when the relationship has been damaged. If Christ loves the church, his wayward bride, and continually woos her back from her spiritual adulteries, how much more should you woo back your wife after a disagreement when half the time it will be your fault anyway? It is always 100 percent the church's fault. And it is never 100 percent your wife's fault. So if you come and tell me that you have big problems in your marriage–"She doesn't respect me, doesn't look good anymore, won't have sex, is hyper-critical, puts the children ahead of me, doesn't support my decisions, spends too much, criticizes me in front of others, worries constantly, has no self-discipline, watches too much TV, keeps the house as clean as a frat party, is too focused on her career, too moody, too demanding, never on time, never prays, and won't admit she's wrong. What do I do, Pastor?"–I will tell you to love your wife as Christ loved the church. Be a man. Be a spiritual leader. Repair the breach.

Husbands, sacrifice for your wives. Perhaps the most important thing for your marriage is that you understand the doctrine of the atonement. Jesus died for the church. Your leadership as a husband is a self-sacrificing leadership.

This can mean little things. Coming home early. Taking care of the kids. Participating joyfully in something she really likes to do. Overlooking an offense. Running errands. Fixing something around the house. Cleaning up the house when she's gone.

And loving your wife can entail bigger sacrifices. You may need to forfeit climbing the corporate ladder in order to be a decent husband. You may be called upon to give up your hopes and dreams to take care of your wife after she has a stroke some day. You may sacrifice the big house or the best neighborhood and live at a lower lifestyle so your wife can stay home with the kids.

Chrysostom, writing in the fourth century, counsels husbands to lay down their lives in love for their wives: "Yea, even if it shall be needful for thee to give thy life for her, yea, and to be cut into pieces ten thousand times, yea, and to endure and undergo any suffering whatever,—refuse it not. Though thou shouldest undergo all this, yet wilt thou not, no not even then, have done anything like Christ" (EN 24).

Finally, husbands, care for your wives. Verse 28 applies the command to love your neighbor as yourself to the marriage relationship: "In the same way husbands should love their wives as their own bodies." Therefore, feed and care for your wife as Christ does for the church.

Provide for her as for your own body. Take care of her needs for food, clothing, and security. There is no law which says the wife cannot make more than the husband, but there is this command for husbands to feed and care for their wives. Your wife should feel secure in your provision and protection of her.

Cherish her as your own body. She is not merely your partner. She is your other half, your own flesh and bone. You don't abuse your body (hopefully). You build up, protect, and nourish it. Likewise, cherish and care for your wife. Colossians 3:19 says, "Husbands, love your wives, and do not be harsh with them." You should just as easily treat your wife harshly as you should punch yourself in the face. "The man who does not love his wife," Calvin says, "is a monster" (EN 25).

The way some guys talk to their wives is unbelievable. They belittle them. They're short, critical, sarcastic, insensitive. I don't care if you are newly married or you've been going at this since before WWII–I don't care what generation you're from–husbands should not be harsh with their wives. Not physically, not verbally. The man who feels like a man because he puts his woman in her place is no man. And he is certainly no Christ.

Maybe there is something right in all those chivalry stories about the man fighting for the honor of the woman, defending her to the last, treating her like a queen. In the book *A Return to Modesty,* Wendy Shalit (not a Christian by the way) comments on the quaint etiquette rules from the past. Rules like "a man always opens a door for a woman...a man carries packages or suitcases for a woman...a man rises when a woman comes into the room...a man also rises when a woman leaves the table...a man rises to speak to a woman or to be introduced to her...If a woman drops her glove in the street, you'd certainly pick it up...It is not particularly charming, incidentally, to race a woman, young or old, for a vacant seat. Tip your hat when you're thanked, and take care to keep the whole thing impersonal so that it doesn't look as if you have ulterior motives." Shalit acknowledges that "one can certainly criticize these rules as sexist, and many have." But she continues, "The simple fact is that a man who observed all of the above rules was a man who treated a woman with respect, a man who was incapable of being boorish. He was too busy doing things to be boorish. This is why I doubt that if men are taught to relate courteously to women, women would suddenly be thrown out of all the professions, as some contend. Maybe, on the contrary, it would be much easier for the sexes to work together. Perhaps we wouldn't have to waste so much time with sexual harassment lawsuits. In the old view, *if you weren't considerate to women, you weren't really a man*" (EN 26).

If it's not a bad idea for men in general to treat other women with care and kindness, how much more so for our own wives. D.L. Moody once remarked, "If I wanted to find out whether a man was a Christian, I wouldn't ask his minister. I would go

146

and ask his wife. If a man doesn't treat his wife right, I don't want to hear him talk about Christianity." What do you think? Would you feel comfortable putting your wife down as a reference on your Christian resume? Throw out all the ways our culture confuses love with feelings and euphoria, could your wife look you in the eye and say with all sincerity and tenderness, "Honey, you love me well...like Christ does the church?"

The End of the Matter: God's Glory

And so I end where this passage ends, with the analogy between Christ and the church. If wives do not submit to their husbands as to the Lord, and husbands do not love their wives as Christ loved the church and gave himself up for her, how does the analogy work in verse 32? Marriage is a picture of Christ and the church. If there is no distinction in roles, no ordering, no self-sacrificing headship, no joyful submission, we are left with Christ and Christ or the church and the church.

Brothers and sisters, God is trying to show something in your marriage. If we disallow any gender-based distinctions, we are not allowing to shine forth the very heart of marriage itself. Yes, God created marriage for companionship, and for sex, and for children, but most of all, he created marriage to reveal this profound mystery of Christ and the church. This is a high calling, His plan is for a watching world to look at husband and wife and see such gentle, joyful submission and such self-denying, loving leadership that it gets a picture of the beauty that is the relationship between Christ and his church. Nothing less than God's full glory is at stake.

THE SLIPPERY SLOPE FROM EGALITARIANISM TO HOMOSEXUALITY

I freely admit that people do not always slide down slippery slopes. I just as gladly acknowledge that I know many individuals who support the ordination of women who are also steadfast in their rejection of homosexual ordination and behavior. Many egalitarians oppose the ordination of homosexuals and firmly reject the homosexual lifestyle. I am in no way suggesting that all egalitarians find homosexual behavior acceptable. But there is a slippery slope from one to the other.

Consider two different "connections" between egalitarianism and homosexual advocacy. The first connection is based on hermeneutics. The approach to Scripture that allows for a non-normative reading of Paul's statements about women is similar to the approach that allows for homosexual behavior.

There is a connection in the way in which an argument is made for the ordination of women based on calling and giftedness and the way in which an argument is made for acceptance of homosexuality based on calling and personhood. Moreover, in both cases new "discoveries" in the original languages are needed to justify overturning the church's long-held position.

On a popular level, at least, the justification for homosexuality and women's ordination often sound the same. I've heard it said, "You know, there's really only a few isolated texts that people use to restrict women's roles, and even these texts are disputed. The passages in 1 Corinthians are clearly cultural (they mention head coverings after all). And the instructions in 1 Timothy have nothing to do with proper authority. It's all about uneducated women usurping authority and teaching what is false. And don't forget about Jesus. He never restricted women's roles. He empowered them and included them. Sure, in a few places the Bible seems to uphold role distinctions, but new word studies have helped us realize that when Paul used 'head' he really meant 'source,' and when he talked about 'authority' he meant 'domineering.' Besides, Galatians 3:28 says there is no male or female in Christ Jesus. We are all one. When we will catch up with the Bible's liberating notion of equality?"

This is not much different from the arguments I often hear made in support of homosexual behavior. "You know, there's really only a few isolated texts that ever condemn homosexuality and even these texts are disputed. The story of Sodom and Gomorrah had nothing to do with committed homosexual relationships. The two passages in Leviticus can't be taken seriously because look at all the other cultural commands in those chapters. And when you come to the New Testament, the main thing you see is Jesus loving the outcasts and marginalized in society. He never condemned homosexuals, but included everyone. Sure, Paul seems to mention homosexuality in a few places, but recent word studies have shown that he probably was talking about pederasty. He only condemned certain types of homosexual behavior. He never said anything negative about those with a homosexual orientation in committed relationships. Besides, Galatians 3:28 says there is no male or female in Christ Jesus. We are all one. When we will catch up with the Bible's liberating notion of equality?" Admittedly, scholars will articulate a more careful presentation, but to many people in the pews, once one argument is accepted, it will be hard to convince them that the other argument doesn't have merit as well.

But the connection between egalitarianism and homosexual advocacy is not only hermeneutical, it is also historical. There is good evidence indicating that the embracing of egalitarianism in one generation often leads to the embracing of homosexuality in the next. David W. Jones, in an article in *The Journal For Biblical Manhood & Womanhood* (EN 27), traces the road from egalitarianism to homosexuality in four different organizations: the Evangelical Women's Caucus (EWC), the Presbyterian Church (USA), the Evangelical Lutheran Church in America (ELCA), and the United Methodist Church (UMC). In each case, the institution drifted over the decades from accepting women in all roles to accepting homosexual behavior.

The Evangelical Women's Caucus (EWC) was born out of the group Evangelicals for Social Action and later became an independent parachurch organization in 1975. Through the 1970s and early 80s, the EWC championed a number of "women's issues," from the Equal Rights Amendment to inclusive Bible translations, and, obviously, the ordination of women. In 1986, a group within the EWC known as "Lesbians and Friends" brought before the entire body a resolution affirming and embracing homosexuality. The resolution passed by a large margin. Over the next two years a more conservative group, rejecting homosexuality, splintered off from the EWC and formed Christians for Biblical Equality (CBE).

The PC(USA), has held, at least in some degree, to an egalitarian view of gender for quite some time. Over these years, the General Assembly has made unequivocal statements condemning homosexuality as sin and prohibiting its ministers from practicing homosexuality and performing homosexual marriages/unions. By 1978, however, the General Assembly showed signs of changing its tune. First came a resolution encouraging love and outreach toward the homosexual community, not in itself a bad thing. Then a 1987 resolution called for the elimination of anti-sodomy laws and discrimination based on orientation. Over the ensuing years, largely through the Women's Ministries Program Area, several pockets in the denomination have been outspoken in their approval of homosexuality. In 1998, the National Network of Presbyterian College Women began producing resources promoting lesbianism. A year later, the Women's Ministries Program Area gave their Woman of Faith award to a full-time homosexual lobbyist. Currently, the group More Light Presbyterians is one of the most adamant voices calling for the full acceptance of homosexuality in all aspects of church life. What began as a concern for women's rights has drifted into homosexual advocacy. As past PC(USA) Moderator (2001) Jack Rogers has stated approvingly, "I believe if we read the Bible in the same way we learned to read it in order to accept the equality of...women, we will be forced to the conclusion that gay and lesbian people are also to be accepted as equal."

The track in the ELCA is like that in the PC(USA). The ELCA formed in 1988 as a merger of three Lutheran denominations. An egalitarian view of gender roles dominated the three partnering groups. The ELCA does not have an official stance on homosexuality, but prior to the merger the separate bodies were on record as cautiously opposed to homosexual behavior. In recent years, however, the full acceptance of the homosexual lifestyle has been encouraged, as per the Presbyterians, through the denomination's women's issues agencies. The head of the ELCA Commission for Women steering committees sees homosexual rights as the next front in the war against gender distinctions: "We are committed to a thorough approach to address sexism in our church–sexism in the broadest sense, including sexism against women and girls, against people who are gay or lesbian, and including the ways in which sexism distorts boys' and men's lives."

Similarly, the UMC shows signs of moving in a direction toward the approval of homosexual behavior. The Methodist church has a long history of women in leadership roles. They are proud of their stance against "sexist discrimination." For many in the UMC, this anti-discrimination stance now embraces homosexuality. Some ministers within the denomination are arguing that "discrimination against the homosexual seeking ordination is as immoral or illegal as discrimination for reasons of gender." Another pastor described "the movement for the inclusion of gays and lesbians [as] a continuation of the civil rights struggles of other groups...[including] women."

The point in these historical portraits is not to link everyone in favor of women's ordination with the pro-homosexual movement. But the slope is a slippery one and institutions have fallen down it before. The same sort of reasoning that denies any gender distinctions in ministry has been used historically to deny the importance of gender in sexuality altogether.

APPENDIX 3

THE DANVERS STATEMENT (EN 28) THE COUNCIL OF BIBLICAL MANHOOD AND WOMANHOOD

Rationale

We have been moved in our purpose by the following contemporary developments which we observe with deep concern:

1. The widespread uncertainty and confusion in our culture regarding the complementary differences between masculinity and femininity;
2. the tragic effects of this confusion in unraveling the fabric of marriage woven by God out of the beautiful and diverse strands of manhood and womanhood;
3. the increasing promotion given to feminist egalitarianism with accompanying distortions or neglect of the glad harmony

portrayed in Scripture between the loving, humble leadership of redeemed husbands and the intelligent, willing support of that leadership by redeemed wives;

4. the widespread ambivalence regarding the values of motherhood, vocational homemaking, and the many ministries historically performed by women;

5. the growing claims of legitimacy for sexual relationships which have Biblically and historically been considered illicit or perverse, and the increase in pornographic portrayal of human sexuality;

6. the upsurge of physical and emotional abuse in the family;

7. the emergence of roles for men and women in church leadership that do not conform to Biblical teaching but backfire in the crippling of Biblically faithful witness;

8. the increasing prevalence and acceptance of hermeneutical oddities devised to reinterpret apparently plain meanings of Biblical texts;

9. the consequent threat to Biblical authority as the clarity of Scripture is jeopardized and the accessibility of its meaning to ordinary people is withdrawn into the restricted realm of technical ingenuity;

10. and behind all this the apparent accommodation of some within the church to the spirit of the age at the expense of winsome, radical Biblical authenticity which in the power of

the Holy Spirit may reform rather than reflect our ailing culture.

Purposes

Recognizing our own abiding sinfulness and fallibility, and acknowledging the genuine evangelical standing of many who do not agree with all of our convictions, nevertheless, moved by the preceding observations and by the hope that the noble Biblical vision of sexual complementarity may yet win the mind and heart of Christ's church, we engage to pursue the following purposes:

1. To study and set forth the Biblical view of the relationship between men and women, especially in the home and in the church.
2. To promote the publication of scholarly and popular materials representing this view.
3. To encourage the confidence of lay people to study and understand for themselves the teaching of Scripture, especially on the issue of relationships between men and women.
4. To encourage the considered and sensitive application of this Biblical view in the appropriate spheres of life.
5. And thereby
   – to bring healing to persons and relationships injured by an inadequate grasp of God's will concerning manhood and womanhood,

– to help both men and women realize their full ministry potential through a true understanding and practice of their God-given roles,

– and to promote the spread of the gospel among all peoples by fostering a Biblical wholeness in relationships that will attract a fractured world.

Affirmations

Based on our understanding of Biblical teachings, we affirm the following:

1. Both Adam and Eve were created in God's image, equal before God as persons and distinct in their manhood and womanhood (Gen. 1:26-27, 2:18).

2. Distinctions in masculine and feminine roles are ordained by God as part of the created order, and should find an echo in every human heart (Gen. 2:18, 21-24; 1 Cor. 11:7-9; 1 Tim. 2:12-14).

3. Adam's headship in marriage was established by God before the Fall, and was not a result of sin (Gen. 2:16-18, 21-24; 3:1-13; 1 Cor. 11:7-9).

4. The Fall introduced distortions into the relationships between men and women (Gen. 3:1-7, 12, 16).

    – In the home, the husband's loving, humble headship tends to be replaced by domination or passivity; the wife's intelligent, willing submission tends to be replaced by usurpation or servility.

- In the church, sin inclines men toward a worldly love of power or an abdication of spiritual responsibility, and inclines women to resist limitations on their roles or to neglect the use of their gifts in appropriate ministries.

5. The Old Testament, as well as the New Testament, manifests the equally high value and dignity which God attached to the roles of both men and women (Gen. 1:26-27; 2:18; Gal. 3:28). Both Old and New Testaments also affirm the principle of male headship in the family and in the covenant community (Gen 2:18; Eph 5:21-33; Col 3:18-19; 1 Tim 2:11-15).

6. Redemption in Christ aims at removing the distortions introduced by the curse.

- In the family, husbands should forsake harsh or selfish leadership and grow in love and care for their wives; wives should forsake resistance to their husbands' authority and grow in willing, joyful submission to their husbands' leadership (Eph. 5:21-33; Col. 3:18-19; Tit. 2:3-5; 1 Peter 3:1-7).

- In the church, redemption in Christ gives men and women an equal share in the blessings of salvation; nevertheless, some governing and teaching roles within the church are restricted to men (Gal. 3:28; 1 Cor. 11:2-16; 1 Tim. 2:11-15).

7. In all of life Christ is the supreme authority and guide for men and women, so that no earthly submission–domestic, religious, or civil–ever implies a mandate to follow a human authority into sin (Dan. 3:10-18; Acts 4:19-20; 5:27-29; 1 Peter 3:1-2).

8. In both men and women a heartfelt sense of call to ministry should never be used to set aside Biblical criteria for particular ministries (1 Tim. 2:11-15; 3:1-13; Tit. 1:5-9). Rather, Biblical teaching should remain the authority for testing our subjective discernment of God's will.

9. With half the world's population outside the reach of indigenous evangelism; with countless other lost people in those societies that have heard the gospel; with the stresses and miseries of sickness, malnutrition, homelessness, illiteracy, ignorance, aging, addiction, crime, incarceration, neuroses, and loneliness, no man or woman who feels a passion from God to make His grace known in word and deed need ever live without a fulfilling ministry for the glory of Christ and the good of this fallen world (1 Cor. 12:7-21).

10. We are convinced that a denial or neglect of these principles will lead to increasingly destructive consequences in our families, our churches, and the culture at large.

Endnotes

1. On this matter, scholars on both sides voice agreement. In *Discovering Biblical Equality*, for example, Pierce and Groothuis write, "Though we speak strongly in favor of unity, points of agreement and dialogue, it must be noted at the start that *we see no middle ground on this question.* The notion of complementarity is helpful and must be pursued, but two essential questions remain. Are all avenues of ministry and leadership open to women as well as men, or are women restricted from certain roles and subordinated to male authority on the basis of gender alone? Likewise, do wives share equally with husbands in leadership and decision making in marriage, or does the husband have a unique responsibility and privilege to make final decisions, based on his gender

alone? The answers to these questions will continue to distinguish clearly between the male leadership and gender equality positions" (17, emphasis added).

2. These questions are similar to those offered by J. Robertson McQuilken in "Problem of Normativeness" in Earl D. Radmacher and Robert D. Preus, eds. *Hermeneutics, Inerrancy, and the Bible* (Grand Rapids: Zondervan, 1984), 222ff.

3. *Commentaries on the Book of Genesis, Vol. I* (Grand Rapids: Baker, 1979), 133.

4. *Genesis,* 130.

5. I first discovered this connection in "Male-Female Equality and Male Headship: Genesis 1-3" by Raymond C. Ortlund, Jr. in *Recovering Biblical Manhood and Womanhood,* 108-9.

6. See for example Grudem, *Evangelical Feminism & Biblical Truth,* 201-11, 544-99. After looking up over 2000 uses of *kephale* in ancient Greek literature from the eighth century BC through the fourth century AD, Grudem has yet to find, nor, he maintains, has anyone else found, "one text in ancient Greek literature where a person is called the *kephale* of another person or group *and that person is not the one in authority over that person or group*" (202). Grudem also makes the important observation that although "source" can be a legitimate translation of *kephale*, there

are no examples where *kephale* means "source *without* authority."

7. Calvin, *Institutes of the Christian Religion* (Louisville: Westminster John Knox Press, 1960), I.xiii.24; emphasis added.

8. It has been my experience, in this country anyways, that the refusal to take the husband's last name is often a statement of protest against a traditional understanding of male headship. But we must allow for exceptions. For example, author Elisabeth Elliot (a staunch complementarian) still writes as Elisabeth Elliot even though her current husband's last name is not Elliot. To change her name for her books would only confuse her readers, not to mention frustrate the publisher who wouldn't sell as many books!

9. This brief reconstruction of Ephesus is indebted to S.M. Baugh's "A Foreign World: Ephesus in the First Century" in *Women in the Church* (1995), 13-52.

10. See S.M. Baugh, "The Apostle Among the Amazons," *Westminster Theological Journal* 56:1 (Spring 1994), 153-71.

11. Several leading egalitarians (e.g., I. Howard Marshall, Craig Keener, William Webb, Kevin Giles) have come to the same conclusion that the infinitives (to teach, to exercise authority) must be positive/positive or negative/negative. Not surprisingly, they tend to see the force as negative instead of positive. Cf *Women in the Church* (2005), 53-84.

12. See H. Scott Baldwin, "A Difficult Word" in Women in the Church (1995), 65-80 and Appendix 2, 269-305 in the same book. The appendix cites and translates over 80 uses of *authenteo* in ancient Greek literature. The negative meaning "to domineer" or "to play the tyrant" occurs once in Baldwin's findings in a sermon by the church Father John Chrysostom (390 A.D.). His use of the word is hyperbolic and clearly within a complementarian framework.

> "To love therefore is the husbands' part, to yield is theirs. If then each one contributes his own part, all stands firm. For from being loved, the wife too becomes affectionate; and from her being submissive, the husband becomes gentle. And see how in nature also it hath been so ordered, that the one should love, the other obey. For when the governing party loves the governed, then every thing stands fast. Love from the governed is not so requisite, as from the governing to the governed; for from the other obedience is due. For that the woman hath beauty, and the man desire, shews nothing else than that for the sake of love it hath been made so. Do not therefore, because thy wife is subject to thee, *act the despot (authentei)*; nor because thy husband loveth thee, be thou puffed up. For this cause hath He subjected her to thee, that she

may be loved the more. For this cause He hath made thee to be loved, O wife, that thou mayest easily bear thy subjection" (*Women in the Church* [1995], 286).

13. The ministry and giftedness of the entire church can be summarized as word and deed. "For I will not venture to speak of anything except what Christ has accomplished through me to bring the Gentiles to obedience—by word and deed" (Rom. 15:18). "And whatever you do, in word or deed, do everything in the name of the Lord Jesus, giving thanks to God the Father through him" (Col. 3:17). "As each has received a gift, use it to serve one another, as good stewards of God's varied grace: whoever speaks, as one who speaks oracles of God; whoever serves, as one who serves by the strength that God supplies—in order that in everything God may be glorified through Jesus Christ. To him belong glory and dominion forever and ever. Amen" (1 Peter 4:10-11).

14. Quoted in Grudem, *Evangelical Feminism and Biblical Truth*, 343-44.

15. Chrysostom, preaching in the fourth century, explained the marriage passage in Ephesians 5 and the slavery passage in Ephesians 6 in very different terms. On why wives should submit to their husbands, he writes, "Because when they are in harmony, the children are well brought up, and the domestics are in good order, and neighbors, and friends, and relations enjoy

the fragrance...And just as when the generals of an army are at peace with one another, all things are in due subordination...so, I say, it is here. Wherefore, saith he, 'Wives, be in subjection unto your husbands, as unto the Lord' (*Nicene and Post-Nicene Fathers, Volume 13* [Peabody, MA: Hendriksen, 2004], 143). Chrysostom assumes submission in marriage to be an unqualified good. But when it comes to slavery in Ephesians 6, he comments, "But should anyone ask, whence is slavery, and why it has found entrance into human life...I will tell you. Slavery is the fruit of covetousness, of degradation, of savagery; since Noah, we know, had no servant, nor had Abel, nor Seth, no, nor they who came after them. The thing was the fruit of sin, of rebellion against parents" (159). Clearly, Chrysostom's approach to slavery is much different than to submission. Headship and submission in marriage was self-evident to him (as it would be in the church for another 1500 years), even when the justification for the institution of slavery was not.

16. *First Things,* April 2003, 42.

17. Susan Foh puts it this way: "For a woman who feels she has the call, an examination of the Bible should show her that her feelings have misled her...She may have certain gifts that seemingly qualify her (by the world's reasoning) for the ministry, such as gifts for teaching, public speaking, exegesis, and counseling. The

Holy Spirit does give such gifts to women, and it is wrong for the church to waste them. But they should not be employed in the office of elder... Women might have the gift of teaching, but women would never be given the gift of being pastor-teacher" (*Women and the Word of God* [Phillipsburg, NJ: Presbyterian and Reformed, 1979], 245.

18. In some denominations, adopting a complementarian position, or any position, is complex. In my denomination, the Reformed Church in America, women are permitted to hold any office, but our Book of Church Order provides room for disagreement on the question of ordination. No member shall be penalized for supporting or objecting to the ordination of women. I take this to mean that my church can preach and even put in writing a complementarian statement, but we cannot disallow women from serving in office, nor can we disallow those who support such a position. In the PC(USA), taking a formal complementarian position is technically impossible. Congregations are required to elect women elders, and since the 1975 Kenyon case, officeholders who oppose the ordination of women cannot be ordained and installed.

19. *Women in the Church* (2005), 154.

20. "The Essence of Femininity: A Personal Perspective" in *Recovering Biblical Manhood and Womanhood*, 394.

21. This sermon is a revised version of two sermons given at University Reformed Church in East Lansing, Michigan on March 20 and April 3, 2005.

22. http://www.foxnews.com/printer_friendly_story/0,3566,124885,00.html (accessed July 7, 2004).

23. In an interview with *Christianity Today*, W. Bradford Wilcox, sociologist and author of *Soft Patriarchs, New Men: How Christianity Shapes Fathers and Husbands,* argues that, "Compared to the average American family man, evangelical Protestant men who are married with children and attend church regularly spend more time with their children and their spouses. They also have the lowest rates of domestic violence of any group in the United States. Journalists such as Steve and Cokie Roberts and Christian feminists such as James and Phyllis Alsdurf have argued that patriarchal religion leads to domestic violence. My findings directly contradict their claims" (August 2004, 44).

24. *Nicene and Post-Nicene Fathers, Volume 13* (Peabody, MA: Hendriksen, 2004), 144.

25. *Commentary on Ephesians* (Grand Rapids: Baker, 1993), 322.

26. *A Return to Modesty* (New York: The Free Press, 1999), 144-45, emphasis added.

27. Fall 2003, 5-19. All quotations are from Jones' article.

28. In addition to being found in print in a number of different places, The Danvers Statement can be accessed online at www.cbmw.org.

To order additional copies of

FREEDOM
AND
BOUNDARIES

Call:

1-877-421-READ (7323)

or please visit our web site at
www.pleasantword.com

Also available at:
www.amazon.com
and
www.barnesandnoble.com

Printed in the United States
46231LVS00001B/103-198